C000079686

More ODD CORNERS *of the* SOUTHERN *from the Days of Steam*

Plate 1: Spades are trumps on the skyline at the country end of **Faversham**. A forest of LCDR finials, balance arms and SR semaphores are mounted on the top platform of an LCDR lattice gantry, while SR Westinghouse shunting discs adorn the lower platform. New colour-light signals are about to replace this majestic array. Meanwhile, rebuilt 'West Country' class Pacific No. 34025 *Whimple* heads a train of Bulleid stock, preparing to depart for the Thanet line. Retirement is nigh for the elderly crewmen – taking water, inspecting the 'motion' or simply looking on. The immaculate water-crane and brazier are also coming to the end of their working life.

More ODD CORNERS *of the* SOUTHERN *from the Days of Steam*

ALAN POSTLETHWAITE

SUTTON PUBLISHING

First published in 2001 by
Sutton Publishing Limited · Phoenix Mill
Thrupp · Stroud · Gloucestershire · GL5 2BU

Copyright © Alan Postlethwaite, 2001

All rights reserved. No part of this publication may be reproduced, stored in a retrieval system,
or transmitted, in any form, or by any means, electronic, mechanical, photocopying,
recording or otherwise, without the prior permission of the publisher and copyright holder.

Alan Postlethwaite hereby asserts the moral right to be identified as the author of this work.

British Library Cataloguing in Publication Data
A catalogue record for this book is available from the British Library.

ISBN 0-7509-2709-7

Endpapers: The goods yard and signal box at Chilham, see *plate 95*.

Dedicated to all the friendly railwaymen
who encouraged the author
during the final decade of steam

Typeset in 10/12 pt Palatino.
Typesetting and origination by
Sutton Publishing Limited.
Printed in Great Britain by
J.H. Haynes & Co. Ltd, Sparkford.

Contents

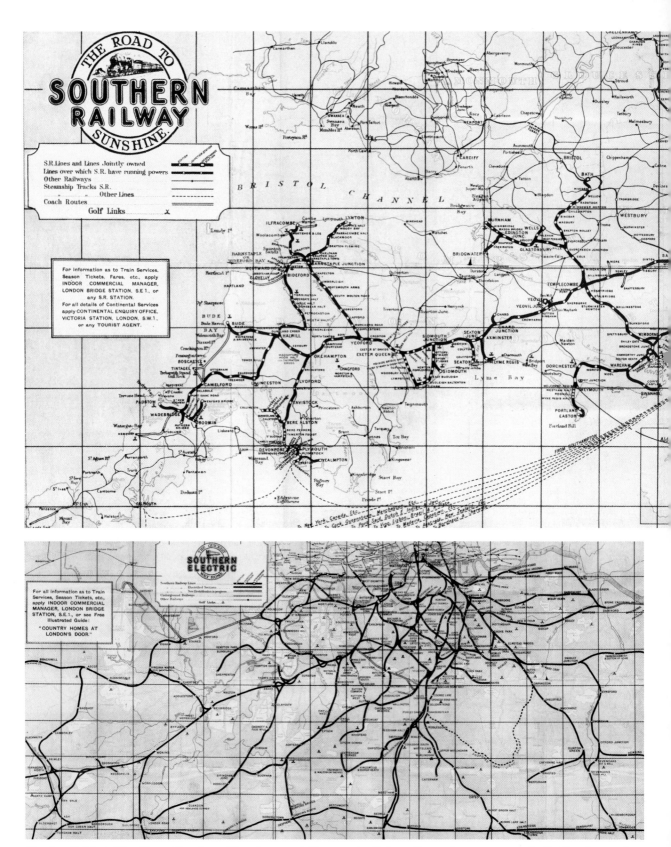

On the *Quickest Way Home* (Southern Electric map, *left*), note the light railway that was never built (Sanderstead to Orpington). Both maps are in colour and include rivers and golf courses (incorrectly labelled 'links').

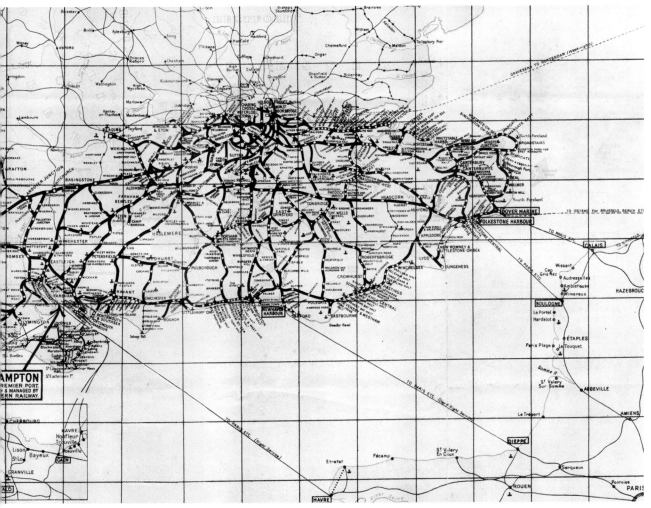

Plate 2: Enjoy the countryside by rail. This well-worn, double-sided pocket map of 1929 shows the Southern Railway system at the peak of its development. On the *Road to Sunshine* (main map, *above*), note the prominence of Southampton Docks, with steamship destinations ranging from the River Plate to Java.

Plate 3: Train arrivals at **Ventnor** were sudden and spectacular from the tunnel entrance of St Boniface Down. With the IWR brick-built signal box so close to the portal, the signalman had to be ready to collect the single-line tablet. He is successful here as LSWR class O2 tank No. 17 *Seaview* emerges into the sunshine. (Alas, the sea could not be viewed from the station!) Note the corrugated roof of the veranda, also the lamp and fire-buckets.

Introduction

The first volume of *Odd Corners of the Southern* (*Ref. 13*) conducted a broad survey of railway features (other than locomotives) to be found during the last decade of steam on BR(S) – the Southern Region of British Railways. This second volume appears in response to the many letters of appreciation requesting more of the same. It seeks to extend the coverage through large-size prints and full captions. Plate numbers are used for cross-references, especially for the many 'composite' photographs which contain material relevant to more than one thematic chapter. The index at the back lists 163 photographic locations. Station locations can be pin-pointed on the two-sided Southern Railway map at the front (*plate 2*).

The geographic scope for this second volume is extended to cover lines not only of the former Southern Railway (SR, 1923–48) but also of certain other lines in the SR area. These are the East Kent Railway (EKR) and the Kent & East Sussex Railway (K&ESR) which remained independent until 1948, and the Somerset & Dorset line which was jointly owned with the LMS. The influence of the GWR is seen from joint workings and various transfers of West of England lines to BR Western Region. Also noticeable is an influx of GWR and LMS locomotives into the Southern Region to replace ageing pre-group stalwarts (pre-1923).

This book identifies the function, appearance and origin of stations, yards, signals, signal boxes, coaches and other railway features. Their origins range from BR, through the golden years of the SR, to the colourful pre-group railway companies – especially the London & South Western (LSWR), the London, Brighton & South Coast (LBSCR) and the South Eastern & Chatham (SECR). We also find remnants of the South Eastern (SER) and of the London Chatham & Dover (LCDR) Railways – those Kentish rivals that merged in 1899 to become the SECR. The smaller constituents of the SR are represented by the Isle of Wight (IWR), the Isle of Wight Central (IWCR) and the Plymouth, Devonport and South Western Junction (PD&SWJR) Railways.

Some 230 photographs and 9 pages of ephemera have been collated into 11 thematic chapters; some include steam trains. For a complete picture of the railway scene, the final chapter is an anthology of locomotives in odd corners – poetry in motion, so to speak. All the photographs were taken by the author between 1958 and 1967. The work is a scrapbook of railway bits and pieces which captured his attention and imagination. While all the pictures were recognised at the time as interesting, the details and origins were not always obvious, requiring subsequent research and some clear thinking. A visit to the National Railway Museum library was invaluable. The most helpful references are listed below.

Some noble attempts have been made over the years to produce mini-encyclopaedias of the Southern, but none comes near to being truly comprehensive. *Reference 1*, for example, is a geographic history, while *Reference 2* is essentially a history of line building and locomotives. C. Hamilton Ellis produced some excellent mechanical histories; others have concentrated on particular lines or specialist topics such as signalling, station architecture and rolling stock (*Refs. 6, 7, 10, 11, 12*). Some books are mainly text, others mainly illustrative. The Middleton Press has produced many bite-size photographic albums covering much of the Southern and comprising summary histories, sample services and maps, line by line and station by station. The nearest overviews of the Southern are probably the two by Whitehouse and Thomas (*Refs 3 and 4*), bristling with short articles on many topics and thoughtfully illustrated.

Each of the above is valuable and interesting, but none is sufficiently thorough to encompass all knowledge on every facet of the history of the Southern. Perhaps the greatest deterrent to a true encyclopaedia of the Southern is that it could never be *fully* completed and validated. There is nothing like the thrill of discovering a booklet or article by an unknown author on some remote railway topic. *Refs 5* and *8* are prime examples of this, describing the route and artefacts of the Surrey Iron Railway and the Isle of Grain Railways.

This book is a small contribution to the great jigsaw of Southern knowledge – a puzzle that we strive to complete, but which will always have some missing pieces. It is intended to be a readable piece of railway archaeology and history which has been reasonably researched. Uncertainties are acknowledged where they are recognised. Doubtless, there are some errors of fact or omission yet to be uncovered.

Factual errors and contradictions are an unfortunate, but inevitable fact of books and articles written by railway enthusiasts. Mitcham station building (*plate 17*) is a case in point, variously described as originating as a private residence or as a railway building. Its true origin remains obscure. One author claims that its arch was added around 1855 for the opening of the Wimbledon & Croydon line and yet the 1850 census names it as 'Archway Houses'.

The prime purpose of this author is to make his photographic collection available to the railway community as a whole, be they historians, locomotive buffs, modellers, preservationists or general enthusiasts. Best efforts have been made to present the pictures clearly in an interesting way and with captions as accurate and full as reasonably possible. It is the pictures themselves that are the main value of the work. Some are unique, either of the artefact itself or within the setting, perhaps with the inclusion of a bicycle, person, poster or road vehicle. Such ancillaries help to portray a full picture of the Southern as it was in the days of steam.

References

1. *A Regional History of the Railways of Great Britain*:
    - Volume 1 *The West Country*, David St John Thomas, 1960.
    - Volume 2 *Southern England*, H.P. White, 1961.
    - Volume 3 *Greater London*, H.P. White, 1963.
2. Marshall, C.F. and Kidner, R.W., *History of the Southern Railway*, Ian Allan, 1963.
3. Thomas, David St John and Whitehouse, Patrick, *SR 150*, Guild Publishing, 1988.
4. Whitehouse, Patrick and Thomas, David St John, *The Great Days of the Southern Railway*, BCA and David St John Thomas, 1992.
5. Bayliss, Derek A., *Retracing the First Public Railway*, Living History Publications, 1981.
6. The Signalling Study Group, *The Signal Box, a Pictorial History and Guide to Designs*, OPC, 1986.
7. Pryer, G., *A Pictorial Record of Southern Signals*, OPC, 1977.
8. Gray, Adrian, *Isle of Grain Railways*, Oakwood Press, 1974.
9. Westcott, Linn H., *Model Railroading with John Allen*, Kalmbach Books, 1981.
10. Harris, Michael, *LNER Carriages*, David St John Thomas, 1994.
11. Gould, David, *Bogie Carriages of the South Eastern & Chatham Railway*, Oakwood Press, 1993.
12. Gould, David, *Maunsell's SR Steam Carriage Stock*, The Oakwood Press, 1978.
13. Postlethwaite, Alan, *Odd Corners of the Southern from the Days of Steam*, Sutton Publishing, 1999.

1 Station Frontages

Station frontages provide first and last impressions for the railway traveller. Stations considered 'important' were generally given impressive frontages, as well as a comprehensive range of passenger facilities, together with the stationmaster's house, which was usually an integral part of the building cluster. The aim was to leave the traveller with a sense of well-being, encouraging him to return again and again. This chapter includes some architectural gems, both large and small. Their styles are described as accurately as possible, with reference to non-railway buildings elsewhere. The LBSCR, LSWR, IWR and the Ventnor West line of the IWCR display the finest collections of architecture.

On the SER and at many remote stations, simple, unpretentious buildings were built in vernacular styles, often little more than huts, either because capital was limited or because passenger comfort and encouragement were considered unimportant. Many urban stations were constrained by the availability and cost of land, resulting in a tiny booking hall with basic passenger facilities. At major terminals, on the other hand, station frontages might be combined with great hotels or offices, often obscuring or diminishing the railway itself.

Contrasting styles of station buildings are presented in this chapter. Most include forecourts for the setting down and picking up of passengers – originally by horse-drawn carriage or cart, but latterly by private motor car, taxi or bus. Parking space was usually modest – indeed, car ownership was exceptional until the end of steam. Passengers would think nothing of walking or cycling miles to the station.

Motor vehicles, people, bicycles, signs and posters add much interest to the station forecourts, contributing to our knowledge of local social history. Thanks are due to Don Pither, author of books on classic cars, for helping to identify the motor vehicles. Thanks also to Merton Local Studies Centre for helping to unravel the story of Mitcham station. A most useful architectural reference book was *A History of Architecture* (nineteenth edition), edited by John Musgrave and published by Butterworths. This has inspired the author to visit some of the original Renaissance buildings in Italy upon which so many railway station buildings were based – known as the Italianate style.

Plate 4: **Canterbury East** is the more important of that city's main line stations, offering fast, direct services to London, rather than via Ashford on the longer SER route. Unusually for the LCDR, the stationmaster's house is long, two-storeyed and in the Italianate style. Its importance is confirmed by fourteen chimney pots, seven motor cars (three of them pre-war) and one bicycle. Note the harmonious proportioning between the chimneys, the hipped roof, the upper-storey 'Georgian' windows and the lower-storey windows with their Roman arches.

Plate 5: The LCDR hotel at the front of **Holborn Viaduct** station was converted into offices during the First World War and was severely bombed during the second. In 1963, it was demolished and replaced by an office block of modern, repetitive, plastic and glass frontage. Bland designs were nevertheless in vogue during the postwar era – the offices were at least light and airy. Clues to the existence of a railway are the smart BR sign and three scalloped sections of canopy. It was always a shock to walk through this smart entrance to find a scene of antiquated ironwork beyond (see *plate 29*). In *Modern Railways* (November 1963), R.J. Marshall likens the experience to crossing from West to East Berlin.

Plate 6: Station buildings on the Ashford West line were more substantial and more elegant than on the LCDR main line through Sole Street. **Harrietsham** has two linked pavilions and an outbuilding, all in red-brick Gothic style with pointed window arches. The canopies too are substantial, with deep LCDR valancing. Building status can be assessed by the number of chimney pots, in this case thirteen. Both the motor-scooter and the Morris 1100 were considered 'trendy' during the early 1960s. See also Bat & Ball station (*plate 91*).

Plate 7: **Faversham**'s main building is north of the tracks, with subway access to the two island platforms. This picture shows the 'backage' rather than the frontage. The central pavilion is a single-storey villa with a series of tall, round-headed windows. It is supported on either side by subsidiary buildings and offices, to create a long, low, restful cluster – less formal than either Canterbury East or Harrietsham. Note the change in platform height (left) due to recent realignments and extensions for impending 12-car EMUs (see also *plate 126*).

Plate 8: **Brasted**'s station building is similar in outline to the upper storey at Canterbury East, having a hipped roof, tall chimneys and windows of Georgian proportions. Here the similarity ends, since this is a typical SER vernacular structure, built cheaply of local timber upon a brick base. For a little-used station, the two canopies are impressive, so too the railings. Here, in 1959, coal traffic remains significant, but the passenger building has been relegated to an unmanned halt, used for games of hide-and-seek. Where is the little girl today?

Plate 9: **Goudhurst** displays an odd contrast of buildings. The booking office is a single-storey hut clad in corrugated steel, whose plainness is relieved only by the entrance canopy and SER-style windows and brick chimneys. The stationmaster, on the other hand, occupies a substantial, three-storey brick house – narrow, but nicely proportioned with steep gables and a balcony over the bay. Together with smaller end-buildings, the row as a whole is neat but sleepy, with pavement grass and just one prospective traveller.

Plate 10: **Kingscote** is a fine example of T.W. Myres' large country stations which he designed for the LBSCR in imitation of the Old English style that Norman Shaw had introduced into Sussex. The two-storey gabled house is substantial, having mullioned windows and one half-face of red tiles. The single-storey booking office has a hipped roof and an elaborate wooden porch – so welcoming to the traveller. The blend of the two halves works well, enhanced by fine brickwork detail. Built at the zenith of LBSCR optimism for new traffic, this investment was largely wasted when traffic failed to grow. It was photographed in 1959, a few years after closure.

Plate 11: **Forest Row** did not close until 1967. Its buildings were substantial, having linked pavilions with tall, elaborate chimneys and a canopy. It is more recognisable as a railway station than the exquisite edifice of Kingscote. The approach road is at the rear of the goods yard, with a rustic wooden fence separating the two. As seen in other yards in Chapter 5 and in *plate 8*, coal was the one remaining freight commodity of any significance. Awaiting the arrival of the next train is a dark green London Transport 'Country Bus' type RT on route 409.

Plate 12: There is nothing pretentious about the frontage of **Queen's Road, Peckham**. The booking office is tucked away in an arch next to a Citroën dealer. Access for maintenance can be a problem on elevated railways – the exterior of the wooden shelter of the Up line looks as though it has never been repainted. The support columns are well braced to prevent buckling, and there is a nice finishing touch of external valancing which few would have noticed from below. The Bedford Dormobile van was considered ultra-modern, *c.* 1960.

Plate 13: No grandeur is apparent at the front of **Littlehampton**. Instead, the station must rely upon green enamelled signs to advertise its existence – both the SR and BR versions are large and clear. Bikes and three taxis await arrivals – the Austin saloons have roof racks, but the London black cab has room for luggage inside.

Plate 14: A batch of LBSCR stations had their main building over the tracks alongside the road bridge. Eridge was one and **Holmwood** was another, seen here. They were convenient for passenger access, but had no forecourt for road vehicles. The stationmaster's house is set apart and private – its two storeys of white walls, in the Italianate style, contrast with the single-storey, red-brick pavilions of the booking office. Two lads discuss options for dog-walking – the long, baggy shorts are reminiscent of Stanley Matthews in his heyday.

Plate 15: The long Italianate frontage of **Tunbridge Wells West** is flanked by the great clock tower (a rival to Big Ben) and by a gabled pavilion on the right. There is a second clock face on the left-hand side and a short gabled pavilion behind the tower. The overall proportions are perfect, so too is the attention to brickwork detail, chimneys and the wooden bell-turret with its weather-vane. All have a subliminal, beneficial impact upon the traveller. Note the similarity of the window arches to those at Forest Row. This LBSCR station was in direct competition with the SER's Central station. Two passengers await taxis while others prefer to walk. Car ownership was uncommon during the early 1960s – two Ford 'runabouts' here are lost in the spacious forecourt.

Plate 16 (*opposite, above*): Charles Barry Junior became architect and surveyor of Dulwich College Estates in 1858. His works included the new college and **North Dulwich** station – one of the architectural gems of the LBSCR. The Grade II listing describes it as Jacobean Revival, but it has no great gables or turrets of that style. Instead, the roofs are low-pitched hipped. Built in red brick with stone dressings, the basic style is Italianate, but with 'Jacobethan' ornamentation. The entrance loggia has three Roman arches on coupled stone columns, similar to the Palazzo dell' Università, Genoa. The clustered chimney pots are Elizabethan, similar to Hatfield House in Hertfordshire. The mullioned windows of the station house (right) are Jacobean, similar to Castle Ashby, Northamptonshire. The balustrades too are Jacobean, similar to Charlton House, Greenwich. The combination of styles works well, giving the impression of a restful, refined villa, although somewhat marred here by the cigarette advertisements on the shop fronts. The chimneys are mostly dummies, since such a small commuting station (with no goods yard) did not need twenty-six fireplaces! The building stands alongside the weight-restricted railway bridge (left). In the modest forecourt are two Morris Minors and an ancient Alvis 'duck-back' convertible.

Plate 17 (*opposite, below*): A contender for the oldest railway station building in the world is at **Mitcham**. Built in about 1803, it may originally have been a residence, possibly two. The *News & Mercury* for Mitcham (5 February 1972) reports that local historian Tom Francis always described it as a 'guard house' for use in connection with the horse-drawn Surrey Iron Railway (which operated from 1803–48). Either way, it became a station building of the Wimbledon & Croydon Railway which opened in 1855 and was shortly absorbed into the LBSCR. It was Grade II listed in 1954 and was later sold off as offices when replaced by a more modest BR booking office. It is an unusual station building – brick-built with a full-width pediment (low-pitched gable), a central archway, a French window above with balcony and raised flower beds to either side. The main road rises to the right to cross the railway. Motor traffic in 1962 comprised an executive Mercedes, a family Ford and a baby Austin.

Plate 18: The long, gabled, white-painted frontage of **Sandown** station is both welcoming and functional. For the summer season of intense holiday traffic, there is plenty of space for road vehicles and a long canopy under which to wait, post a letter or make a phone call. The stationmaster presumably occupied the entire upper storey, an unusual arrangement for a remote station. It looks as though his balcony was glazed to create a south-facing conservatory, no doubt ideal for cacti and succulents. What an idyllic life he must have led!

Plate 19: **Shanklin**'s frontage is also spacious and welcoming with a more traditional arrangement of linked pavilions in red brick. Ornamental features include a pyramidal turret, shaped ridge tiles, Roman window arches and valancing for the long canopy. The parked cars (left to right) are a Humber saloon, a black cab and an Austin Somerset saloon. The 'Heath Robinson' traffic island is a lovely touch, built out of an old tea chest. Compared with Sandown, the advertised price of cheap tickets to London has increased from 20s to 20s 3d.

Plate 20: **Bembridge** provides a further example of the stationmaster living 'over the shop'. The result is a tall, solid rectangular block, but beautifully ornamented with pilasters, fine brickwork in several colours and two clusters of tall 'Tudor' chimneys. At the near end, the single-storey office looks like an extension, but it blends in well, in contrast to the crude, wooden platform canopy which stands out like a sore thumb (see also St Helens in *plate 88*). There is plenty of space for road vehicles, but there is no pavement or roadside canopy. The entrance to the booking office is tiny and obscure and the modern weighing machine looks quite out of place.

Plate 21: Built towards the end of the island's railway mania, the terminus of **Ventnor West** is on a scale and expense out of proportion to its importance. Built of dressed stone with variegated roof tiles and a cockscomb ridge, the tall, square stationmaster's house contrasts with the long single storey of the booking office. The wide, segmental-headed windows are in the Domestic Revival style. The valanced canopy, on the other hand, is pure Victoriana. One is put at ease upon arrival – welcome to the Isle of Wight Central Railway. Sadly, traffic was always light and the branch closed in 1953. A local builder is the new occupier (see also *plate 86*).

Plate 22: The London & Southampton Railway opened in 1838–9 with terminals in Italianate neo-Classical style to the design of Sir William Tite. The frontage of **Southampton Terminus** is stunning – a bold block in Portland stone whose entrance loggia, balustrade, balcony and windows are remarkably similar to La Scala theatre, Milan. The colonnade is over-sized for purists of classicism, but this is a practical railway station, as confirmed by the central clock. The tall entrance offers both a welcome and a sense of dependability. The station closed in the 1960s and was listed Grade II. The former South Western Hotel stands on the right.

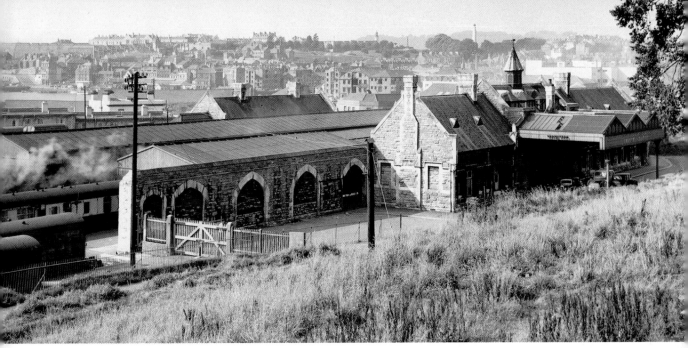

Plate 24 (*above*): In contrast to the classicism at Southampton, the large LSWR terminus of **Plymouth Friary** is less formal. Its main building resembles a pair of tithe barns with a central church turret and a large carriage canopy. This country style is nevertheless welcoming, although the frontage can only be fully appreciated from the grassy hill at the rear. Elegant stone walls and wooden canopies surround the terminal tracks and a secondary building is apparent on the far side. It was a fine place to begin and finish long journeys to Exeter and London.

Plate 25: The GWR station of **Bodmin General** was a branch terminus with a track layout similar to its LSWR competitor. The Great Western, however, offered fast services to Penzance, Plymouth, Exeter and London, with just one change at Bodmin Road. Traffic was therefore the more substantial, as illustrated here with several passengers, a van, a Ford Anglia, a Morris Oxford and a pair of horses. The low-profile, granite, vernacular-style building is similar to that at Bodmin North, but wrapped around the three sides of the terminal end.

Plate 23 (*opposite, below*): The Bodmin & Wadebridge was an early railway, opening in 1834 and taken over by the LSWR in 1845. The line was reconstructed in stages from 1886 and the new **Bodmin North** station was opened in 1895. Its traffic was mainly local, despite later connection to the North Cornwall line at Wadebridge. In vernacular-style, we find a modest, restful, country-branch terminus. The small rectangular granite building has a pleasant blend of colours and a roof profile which is repeated in the substantial platform canopy (see also *plate 62*). A lone passenger approaches through the giant-size wooden gates, but no road traffic is apparent.

Plate 26: **Callington**'s single platform had a magnificent overall wooden roof, but a tiny, crude booking office clad in corrugated steel upon a concrete base. Having no railway competition, frontage magnificence was no doubt deemed unnecessary here by the PD&SWJR. Three slender flues serve the coke stoves. Note the several railway posters and the two six-bar gates which guard the tarred roads to the loco yard and the 'new' goods yard. However, they did not deter the dog who is caught 'doing his business' below the concrete fence.

Plate 27: At **Combpyne**, the stationman's white-painted, two-storey, gabled house looks non-railway. By contrast, the single-storey, red-brick booking office alongside looks purpose-built. The approach is guarded by a wooden hut and white wooden gates upon concrete posts – were they ever closed? Parked on the pavement are an old-fashioned bike, a doll's pram, a pedal-car and three churns for water (delivered by rail). We might well be entering a farm yard – only the four colourful railway posters give the game away (see also *plate 64*).

2 Platform Canopies

This chapter examines the design, construction and appearance of platform canopies, identifying the characteristics of different railway companies, especially the valances. A few canopies extended across the tracks to become train sheds, as at Callington (*opposite*).

Canopies protected people, luggage, parcels, weighing machines, cupboards and seats from the weather, particularly rain and sunshine. They also give partial wind protection, depending upon elevation, platform orientation and the prevailing wind velocity – it always seems to whistle through elevated stations. The LSWR liked to provide a glazed end partition for wind protection, transforming the canopy into a large, open shelter (*plate 58*).

The more conventional shelters were enclosed in timber, except for small windows and a front opening. By providing a door, the shelter became a waiting room, usually with an open hearth or stove for winter heating and perhaps a table for magazines. Since shelters and waiting rooms were generally set back from the platform, they were often provided with canopies. They were temporary refuges, with seats, benches and colourful posters.

The canopy illustrations include a wealth of other railway features and artefacts such as booking offices, station houses, yards, signals, signal boxes, lamp standards, seats, barrows, people, tracks and the occasional train. Here we encounter the steam locomotive for the first time, as well as a few suburban electrics. All are described as appropriate – indeed, canopies are an excellent excuse to wander along the platforms and explore, always an enjoyable experience for enthusiasts. The best-looking stations had a comprehensive design with regard to layout, style and ornamentation. The finest dispositions were works of art, worthy of modelling.

Plate 28: Photographed during modernisation in 1959, **Bromley South** has a spacious cross-track booking office with a hipped roof. A new colour-light gantry is already installed, scaffolding is in place on the cross-corridor and platform canopies are being rebuilt. A workman (left) is working on the glazing of the plain, modern-looking BR canopy, carried on new steel crossbeams which are apparently held up by sky-hooks. Another workman (right) removes the old LCDR canopy and its wooden crossbeams. The original columns and longitudinal lattice beams were retained – a mere sixty-five years old, there was nothing much wrong with them.

Plate 29: **Holborn Viaduct** opened in 1874 with short platforms, sufficient for half-length trains which were divided and rejoined at Herne Hill. In 1925, island platforms 4 and 5 were extended for 8-car EMUs. Platform 1 followed in 1939, obscuring the small engine shed (right). Because of restricted space, the other three platforms remained short and unelectrified, used for parcels, mails and Fleet Street newspaper traffic. Overall, there is an air of antiquity and plainness. Three steel-truss train sheds have clerestories for smoke escapement, but are not originals. The wooden platform canopies, with short valances, are LCDR. The (relocated) island lamp standards are of the straight-fluted LCDR type with a crude SR electric lamp from the 1920s. The station closed in 1990.

Plate 30: St Paul's opened in 1886 and was renamed **Blackfriars** in 1937. Three terminal platforms (right) were used mainly for off-peak train storage. They have overall glass roofs, while the two through lines have an unusual arrangement of trussed arches for canopies. A tall glazed roof covers the concourse at the 'land' end. Wooden platforms extend over half the width of the Thames, reverberating under one's feet and never feeling quite secure. The place was always draughty and 'temporary'. Station staff at least had the comfort of a wooden hut with a stove (centre). Sir Christopher Wren's cathedral soars magnificently above waterfront warehouses.

Plate 31: SR canopies were generally plain with no fancy valancing. Projecting to the south of Eccleston Bridge, **Victoria**'s island platform 1 and 2 has the air of a seaside pier. A single row of posts supports the narrow, wooden canopy, dating from the 1923 rationalisation of the two Victorias. Note the wooden extension to the width of platform 1, added when a parcels bay (to the right) was eliminated after 1923. This right-hand road was originally mixed-gauge to accommodate GWR trains, with a much shorter platform similar to Holborn. On a sunny spring morning, SECR class N Mogul No. 31413 prepares to take empty stock to Eardley sidings via Herne Hill, Tulse Hill and Streatham. Note the SR parcels trolley to carry rear lamps to the buffer-stop end.

Plate 32: **Chatham** has a large cross-track booking office with round-headed windows instead of the square-cornered ones seen at Bromley South. Two island platforms are wide enough for waiting rooms and offices. Their sloping canopies carry short LCDR valancing. In 1959, the platforms were extended for 12-car EMUs, necessitating the closure of both loop lines and the Up goods yard (left) on this tunnel-restricted site. Stopping trains would in future be overtaken by expresses on new loop lines laid between Rainham and Newington. SR art deco concrete lamp standards carry loudspeakers, BR name signs and some non-standard gas-lamp shades.

Plate 33: Ashford's great platforms had comprehensive canopies with SECR valancing. Their end profile resembles an albatross in flight. The SR stop signal (left) with mechanical route indicator is for 'starting back' from the Up loop. SECR 4–4–0 class D1 No. 31489 prepares to restart to Dover with a long train of Bulleid stock and parcels vans, while a tall column of relief steam rises from a Maidstone East train, awaiting departure.

Plate 34: Dunton Green was remodelled in 1881 with a new, curving bay for Westerham branch trains, represented here by Wainwright 0–4–4 class H tank No. 31518. The canopy is non-standard for the SER, having boarding on the underside. The valance, however, is a simple version of the SER machined style, with no holes.

Plate 35: **Herne Bay** has a cantilevered platform canopy, with the valance cut away for a banner repeater signal (which is covered up here). In a rare instance of new SECR building, the station was refurbished in 1915 with new neo-Classical booking halls behind the original offices. The Up block is seen here (left). Note the lattice footbridge. The special train of Maunsell/BR/Pullman coaches is headed by light Pacific No. 34068 *Kenley*.

Plate 36: Some detail of a ridged canopy and a well-weathered wall at **Herne Bay**. The LCDR windows have beautifully finished arches and roundels in coloured bricks. The canopy glazing is superbly effective, although the glass has been replaced with translucent plastic. The suspended cables and pipe are unsightly but necessary.

Plate 37: Platforms 3 and 4 at **London Bridge** have a wide, almost flat island canopy supported on two rows of tubular columns. The *fleurs-de-lys* of the SER valancing are slightly larger than at Strood (*opposite*), but the satisfying 'country craft' effect is the same. In contrast to the busy, twice-daily rush-hours, no passengers are evident as 'West Country' class Pacific No. 34021 *Dartmoor* trundles through with a mid-morning train to the Channel ports. The footbridge is similar to Dartford's (*opposite*), but there is no tarmac on these well-laid flags.

Plate 38: Two patterns of SECR canopy on **Ashford**'s Down platform: tall with an SER arc roof in front of the booking hall (see also *plates 55* and *221*); and a much lower, flat roof along the rest of the platform. The plain, slotted valances are SECR. Note the rectangular, flat-topped brick chimneys on this surprisingly modest, single-storey station building. Parcels are piled high on the platform as a steamy standard 2–6–4 tank No. 80040 shunts a Maunsell utility van on to the rear of a passenger train. See *plate 33* for the SECR canopy end-profile.

Plate 39: In contrast to the plain, slotted valances of the LCDR and SECR, those of the SER were beautifully machined with ornate curves, flats and holes, with many variations of this motif. **Strood** has one of the more intricate patterns, with *fleurs-de-lys* and small circular holes in the longer planks. The canopy roofs are shallow-angled for inward drainage to a central gutter, with a single row of support girders. An EPB train approaches from Rochester while the Maidstone West shuttle waits in the loop. The flagstones are thinly tarmaced.

Plate 40: **Dartford**'s island canopy looks in need of a coat of paint. It has a simple version of SER valancing, with small circular holes. The drainage is outward-flowing to gutters at the edges. On a damp winter's morning, passengers await the next train to Gravesend while EPB motormen and station staff 'put the world to rights'. Note the late-SR art-deco electric lamps and standards, also the lattice footbridge – open-sided but roofed.

Plate 41: Peckham Rye station was built by the LBSCR, encompassing the LCDR line as well its own South London line. The Catford Loop Up canopy displays the heavy baroque style of LBSCR, having 'saw-tooth' valancing and an ornate top edge. A cross-London freight train from Hither Green yard is headed by a grimy SECR 0–6–0 class C No. 31317. Note the longitudinal planking leading to the 'B' signal box (see *plate 167*).

Plate 42: The two island platforms at **East Grinstead** high-level had waiting rooms. Stairs led to the Bluebell station below. The hipped canopies are wide and long with narrow LBSCR valancing. Fairburn 2–6–4 class 4 tank No. 42090 heads a middle-of-the-day service from Victoria to Tunbridge Wells West. The raised section of platform (left) is due to a bridge arch over the low-level lines – another can be seen between the tracks. Although not to RHS standards, the flower bed below the name sign is a pleasant, welcoming gesture.

Plate 44 Some detail of **East Grinstead**'s low-level canopies. Compared with Dorking North (*plate 46*), the underside is unboarded and the brackets are less elaborate, but there is an additional sub-frame for the hipped roof. The valance is a delight, with machined shapes of hearts, clubs and plants in new leaf. Although the front has been cropped for train clearance, the overall effect is quite beautiful. 'Please use our railway!' it cries.

Plate 43: East Grinstead low-level had spacious platforms which swept beneath the bridge of the high-level platforms. The grand Old English style of the station building (right) is reflected in the majestic canopies with their braced backs, low hipped roofs and ornate valances. This fine setting is complemented by a rich backdrop of trees and LBSCR lamp standards to which swan-necks have been added for the Sugg Rochester gas lamps.

Plate 45: **Horam**'s valances are narrow but elaborate. The hipped canopy roofs are apparently lead-covered, supported from the walls and on wooden posts with 45° struts. They complement the Up waiting room (left) and a fine station building in LBSCR Old English style (see *plate 10*). The platforms look immaculately clean and tidy.

Plate 47: Brockley station was joint SER/LBSCR, opened in 1871 to compete with the LCDR's Greenwich Park branch (furthest bridge in picture). The nearest bridge is a public footway with boarded sides (to prevent vandalism). The Down building is single-storey in SER style, but the double canopy is more akin to the LBSCR, having a plain, slotted valance that is in need of a coat of paint. This was an early railway, as evidenced by the many trunk telegraph lines. The 4-EPB train is an off-peak service from Charing Cross to Caterham.

Plate 48: East Croydon station was built by the LBSCR in 1909. This island canopy is wide and heavy-looking with a flat top and a plain, slotted valance. The hexagonal gas lamps are of early SR art-deco type with individual glass panels. Platform 6 is occupied by an Up Oxted train headed by standard 2–6–4 tank No. 80015.

Plate 46 (*opposite*): Detail of the great canopy of **Dorking North**'s island platform. From a row of slender posts spring the most elaborate of brackets. The floral motif tracery looks Jacobean or even Art Nouveau. They support wooden cantilevers which carry the longitudinal roof beams. The valance is of heavy LBSCR type, as already seen at Peckham Rye. Note the emergency tool cupboard, fire buckets, LBSCR seat, wire basket and a wall by the gents', covered in posters. Doris Day and Jack Lemmon are appearing together at the Embassy in *It Happened to Jane*.

Plate 49: Wooden commuting platforms at **Berrylands** were added to the slow lines in 1933. The canopies are cantilevered on steel girders – so plain compared with those at East Grinstead or London Bridge. Coasting through with an Up express from Bournemouth is 'Merchant Navy' class Pacific No. 35002 *Union Castle*.

Plate 50: The smart country station of **Ashtead** is enhanced by sunshine and scattered cumulus. Electrified in 1925 for intensive commuting, a London Bridge to Dorking North service is seen here. The disposition of signal box, level-crossing, station house and single-storey booking offices is delightful. The station was jointly owned and worked by the LBSCR and LSWR. The signal box is of LBSCR in-house design (see also *plate 164*). Resembling an Abbey National Building Society 'umbrella' logo, the canopies are typical of the LSWR in Surrey, having a 30° isosceles triangle in a gabled roof with a central row of wooden support posts. The neat, slotted valances have triangular points which create the illusion of being curved. Note the platform destination boards which slot into the canopy posts.

Plate 51: The vernacular wooden station building at **Lyme Regis** has a corrugated roof. The narrow saw-tooth valance is similar to many on the LBSCR (see *plates 41* and *46*), no doubt chosen by the contractor, rather than by the LSWR. The platform edge has been rebuilt in prefabricated concrete, but the large-wheeled barrows are distinctly LSWR. Adams 4–4–2 radial tank No. 30583 stands proud at the head of a short train of Maunsells.

Plate 52: **Glastonbury and Street** was a remote junction station on the Somerset & Dorset Railway. Great gabled canopies are supported on wooden posts. Fancy valances adorn both the canopies and the booking office. Bargeboards, like rolling waves, bring a touch of the Jacobean. The lattice footbridge is enclosed and there are flower-beds on the platforms. What a philistine act to have closed such an exquisite station.

Plate 53: **Downton**'s plain canopy is a full cantilever with massive girder brackets which spring from the front wall of the booking office. Canopy size is minimal, just sufficient to cover an LSWR seat, a stretcher cupboard and a parcel. A stationman observes the arrival of standard 2–6–0 class 4 No. 76054 with a train from Salisbury.

Plate 54: Opened in 1872, the relocated **Bideford** station has a long, flat-roofed canopy on the Up platform, supported on a row of slender iron columns. The fanciful valance (common in the West Country) is repeated on the LSWR Type 1 signal box, but not on the Down canopy. Ivatt 2–6–2 class 2 tank No. 41294 prepares to take an early train to Barnstaple. The LSWR barley-sugar standard has an unusual swan-neck to the gas lamp.

3 Country Stations and Halts

Hundreds of country stations once served scattered communities – predominantly farming, sometimes with industries. They generated a modest but steady flow of freight and passenger traffic. Indeed, some branch lines were promoted by local communities for their own benefit. With the steady switch to road transport from 1920 onwards, country rail traffic declined inexorably (with the notable exception of coal). Some country stations survived the Beeching closures of the 1960s, becoming commuter stations with large car parks or modern housing estates nearby, but in return they lost their goods yards, steam locomotives, signal boxes, dedicated staff and much of their charm.

Some country stations were built on a grand scale, reflecting the optimism in traffic growth. Wateringbury, Overton and Holmwood are in this category – all on double-track main or secondary lines, with only Overton closing under Beeching. At the other extreme are the low-usage simple wooden, metal or concrete halts of North Hayling, Hurst Green and Cement Mills – all looking temporary, with only Hurst Green surviving to the present day (in rebuilt form). Between these extremes are the 'sensible' stations and halts whose size, design, facilities and comforts were 'just right' for their modest traffic. Sharnal Street, Shapwick, Gunnislake, Sturminster Newton, Bodmin North, Slinfold, Combpyne, Dunsbear and Stoke Junction were all 'sensible' and appropriate for traffic of the early twentieth century, but only Gunnislake survived the road transport revolution.

Charm is the common denominator of these stations and halts. Most were kept in immaculate condition by friendly, loyal staff who took a real pride in their jobs. Who, one wonders, trimmed the hedge at the unmanned halt of Dunsbear? It must have been someone who loved the railway and its stations. It was a pleasure to wait for a train at such places – to sit and absorb the country atmosphere and to marvel that the railway should be there at all.

Plate 55: **Sharnal Street** station building is SER vernacular – of single-storey wooden construction with tall chimney stacks and an arc-roof canopy. When the passing loop was reinstated in 1934, a simple shelter with a modest canopy was added to the Down platform. Its passenger access was via the foreground crossing, lit by an SER oil lamp. Note the platelayers' trolley by the corrugated steel lamp room. On a Bank Holiday service, a pair of SECR class H tanks depart for Allhallows-on-Sea with two push-pull sets. Set 716 is of LBSCR origin.

Plate 56: **Wateringbury** station serves a modest community on the Paddock Wood–Maidstone West branch. It is dominated by the Tudor-style building on the Up side. This extraordinary extravagance is shown off to the full by the SER practice of staggered platforms – linked here by a pre-cast concrete SR-style footbridge. Passing through with a van train from Hoo marshalling yard, during the transition from steam, is Bo-Bo Type 3 diesel-electric No. D6518. It provides a stark contrast to the multiple, steeply pitched, gabled roofs with tall, ornate chimneys. Note the multi-spar trunk telegraph on this early SER line, also the banner repeater signal.

Plate 57: Opened in 1907 at the junction of the East Grinstead and Hever lines, **Hurst Green Halt** had simple wooden platforms. It looks temporary, and indeed it was replaced in 1961 by much longer platforms in concrete, seen on the far side of the road bridge. Until then, facilities comprised wooden benches, corrugated metal shelters and six tall SR electric lamp standards. Concrete cable channels are piled on the Down end-ramp, while a passenger and his lad wait patiently. The leafless ash makes a fine silhouette on the skyline.

Plate 58: Country stations on the main line to Salisbury had substantial buildings but few passengers. At **Overton**, a shelter on the Down platform has a glazed end partition of twenty-five panes, a distinct LSWR feature. (Oh, for such protection at Blackfriars, see *plate 30*.) The signal box is an LSWR Type 1, having a hipped roof, an ornate vent, a tall, brick chimney and a narrow band of windows (echoed on the small room on the Up side). The boarding is horizontal and lapped, built upon a stone base, with a brick lean-to of a later date.

Plate 59: The passing station of **Shapwick** had a simple, wooden, gabled building with a small canopy. It was rebuilt in 1900, following a fire in the adjacent signal box. The new LSWR Type 4 box is located beyond the level-crossing, but it was built on peat bogs with inadequate foundations, causing it to lean. The platforms are SR pre-cast concrete from the 1920s (judging by the pre-cast name signs). The oil lamps may be a mix of S&D and Central Somerset (one of S&D's two original constituents). This line was originally broad-gauge, hence the generous gap between the tracks. Note the water churn on the platform, delivered by rail to this remote outpost.

Plate 60: On top of the world at **Gunnislake**, the island platform accommodates the booking office: a long, single storey and with cantilevered canopies on either side. Passenger access is via the white gates at the right-hand end. Ancillaries include two seats, an SR name sign and three barrows. There are several huts at the far end, together with a lower-quadrant signal of PD&SWJR vintage. Long sidings serve the goods yard, now so quiet. They originally handled minerals from local mines, also goods from a tannery, a pottery and agriculture.

Plate 61: The sleepy country passing station of **Sturminster Newton** on the Central Dorset section of the S&D. The elegant booking office is brick with a steep, gabled roof. The signal box is of LSWR design. Having semi-staggered platforms with no footbridge, the Up platform has the quaint 'Continental' feature of a dip to help passengers step to and from the crossing to the Down platform (towards Bournemouth). The water tank is a delight, built upon a fine stone base. Together with the goods shed (left), they create a gateway effect. Pictorial framing is completed by the LSWR signal post, the telegraph pole and a great backcloth of trees in full leaf.

Plate 62: Although serving Cornwall's county town, **Bodmin North** had a simple 'country terminus' layout with a single platform, a run-round loop and adjacent goods sidings. Sidings to the left and behind the camera were for general storage and locos. Two pleasant 'vernacular' stone buildings are dwarfed by the great LSWR canopy and by the modern bungalows beyond. The SR signal arm is set upon a lattice post of LSWR design. (See also *plate 23*.)

Plate 63: Despite being electrified in 1929, **Holmwood** retains the charm of a fine LBSCR country station, seen here with a Bulleid 4-SUB unit. The enclosed footbridge is adjacent to the cross-track booking office (which is featured in *plate 14*). To the right is the white-painted stationman's house and the goods yard approach road. The signal box is an S&F Type 4 of normal height, but built into the Up platform. It is brick-built with a hipped roof, a stove-pipe, 4x4 windows and boarded top-lights. A wooden closet stands outside. Note the trunk telegraph, an SR art-deco lamp standard and a neatly trimmed privet hedge. The station as a whole looks immaculate.

Plate 64: The peaceful, pastoral setting of **Combpyne**, the only intermediate station on the Lyme Regis branch. Platform facilities comprise one seat, one lamp and a name-board, in contrast to the substantial house, booking office and telegraph pole by the entrance gate (left, seen also in *plate 27*). Passenger access is across the goods siding (which was once a passing loop). Here it holds two BR vans and an LSWR camping coach. The piled sleepers look as good as new, although they do have chair marks. How about a week's rambling holiday here?

Plate 65: The Horsham & Guildford Direct Railway was a contractor's line, taken over by the LBSCR in 1864. Most of its signal boxes were of Saxby & Farmer Type 3b, as seen here at **Slinfold**. A false sense of height is created by the vertical battening, hipped roof and a narrow band of small windows. The enamelled sign is BR. It guards the small goods yard for the bay and coal supplies. The running line is straight and single, flanked by LBSCR wooden signal posts. The station building is large, mainly accommodation for the stationman and his family. Life here would have been simple but pleasant. There was even a wooden catwalk to the signal box.

WHISTLE

Plate 66: **Dunsbear Halt** existed primarily for the workers of the North Devon Clay Company's quarries at Marland Moor (*plate 238*). Facilities on the stone-faced platform comprise a bench, two shelters, a name sign and a neatly trimmed hedge. Train crews would unlock a ground-frame to operate the point and catch-point of the siding. The wooden painted Whistle sign was no doubt for an ungated crossing ahead. The progress of trains in about 1960 could be traced by regular Clyde hoots from the LMS tank engines as they approached the crossings.

Plate 67: **Stoke Junction Halt** was in a bleak and desolate corner of Kent. Passenger facilities comprised a concrete platform and a name sign from the 1920s, together with a wooden shelter and several oil lamps. The crossing-keeper's bungalow looks more hospitable; his squat signal box with a ground-frame can also be seen. The single siding has an SER loading gauge and a neat pile of coal. The site as a whole looks tidy but little-used.

Plate 68: On the Isle of Wight, anyone could buy a ticket to **Cement Mills Halt**, although no trains were advertised to stop there. Facilities for cement workers comprised a short wooden platform, a simple concrete shelter and a crude SR lamp set upon a tall concrete standard. Passenger access to the works was across the sleeper-built crossing. A lock is clearly visible on the ground-frame to operate the siding point and catchpoint.

Plate 69: The simple halt of **North Hayling** comprised a short platform of transverse planks, wooden fencing, a crude bench and a wooden shelter. There is no permanent lighting, but train guards could fix an oil lamp to the post on the right. This bleak location has no sign of civilisation. In fine weather, however, it remains a wonderful, exhilarating line to walk – a natural bird sanctuary with several sea inlets (from the left).

4 Stations Long Closed

Railway stations are closed when they become unneeded and/or uneconomic. Low usage is the most common cause of closure. Another cause is replacement by a larger or more convenient station nearby. The question then arises – what to do with the old station site and its buildings? The longest preserved are often those which are retained for freight, using the old buildings as railway offices and stores. Blackfriars Bridge and Merton Abbey are prime examples of this.

Buildings sold off as businesses or residences may be altered or improved, unless there is a preservation order on them, as at Mitcham (seen in *plate 17*). Buildings adjacent to running lines will certainly need a protective fence from the frequent trains that thunder past, day and night, as seen at Tooting and Smeeth. The saddest closed stations are those which are abandoned and left to decay, like Biddenden and Merstone – probably to be condemned as dangerous and then demolished. The most enigmatic station sites are those sold off and cleared quickly for complete redevelopment, leaving little if any trace of the railway. At Ramsgate Harbour, for example, the only remaining evidence of the former railway is the tunnel portal; there is no trace of the magnificent LCDR beach-terminus.

Examples of each are described and contrasted in this chapter – the magnificent, the curious and the sad, with closure dates ranging from 1885 to 1956. They are nostalgic reminders of the pre-group railways in their heyday – buoyed by Victorian optimism and driven by fierce competition to capture as much as possible of the growing market for travel. Closed stations are often haunted by their former passengers, train crews, station staff and builders. The buildings that survive are a fine tribute to their craftsmen: Victorian bricklayers, carpenters and general navvies whose products were designed and built to last a hundred years or more.

Plate 70: The original (1864) LCDR terminus at Blackfriars was on the south side of the Thames and was generally known as **Blackfriars Bridge**. It became goods-only when St Pauls station opened in 1885. Three-quarters of a century later, the south end of the old train shed holds just two wagons. SECR 4–4–0 class E1 No. 31507 is a temporary visitor, blowing off steam and ready to take over the running of an RCTS rail-tour from Liverpool Street. The yard is segregated from the running lines by a fence of SR concrete posts, which also carry cables. Cart access to the yard was via a cobbled ramp on the left. The poster is for dark rum.

Plate 71: The Tooting, Merton & Wimbledon Railway was opened in 1868, jointly owned by the LSWR and LBSCR. It had two approaches to Wimbledon, thus obviating the need to reverse suburban steam trains which ran to Ludgate Hill and London Bridge. The section through Merton Abbey was closed to passengers in 1929, eclipsed by the Northern Line's extension to Morden. It remained open for freight until 1968, serving factories, general goods yards and coal yards. Photographed in 1962, the brick platforms of **Merton Abbey** look in good condition, although grassy. The LBSCR-style building had become part-goods office and part-residence.

Plate 73: The platform rooms of **Blackfriars Bridge** station were graceful and substantial, elegantly faced in Portland stone. The wooden platform is low-level, with a wide staircase from Southwark Street. Closed in 1885, subsequent acts of architectural vandalism include two dilapidated door canopies and a flue from a stove in the goods station below. Fire fighting provisions comprise one bucket and an extinguisher. One could feel important arriving here from Dover, but the cost of this fine, short-lived terminus (and of the Metropolitan Extension as a whole) was a major cause of LCDR financial impoverishment from which it never recovered.

Plate 72 (*opposite*): **Tooting** was a joint LSWR/LBSCR station on the direct spur to Wimbledon, via Haydon's Lane. Opened in 1868, it closed in 1895, replaced by a new junction station to serve the Merton Abbey spur. The junction here was severed in 1934. The new station is in the background, also the former junction signal box and new buffer stops of Tooting goods yard (right). The original station building became a residence with wire fencing along the edge of the Up platform. It has a restful cottage style – single-storey, brick-built, gabled and bayed. As with Smeeth (*plate 74*), it makes a fine place to live if you don't mind frequent trains. Electrified in 1929, EMU services ran from Holborn Viaduct via Wimbledon and Sutton to West Croydon.

Plate 74: **Smeeth** station, a few miles west of Ashford, opened in 1851 and closed in 1954. Seven years later, little remains of the Up platform – reduced to a bank of earthy rubble. The simple wooden shelter remains in tact, however, having unusual round-headed window frames. The buildings are also unusual for the SER, comprising of three single-storey linked pavilions. They had become a residential bungalow, complete with a TV aerial and an overhead power supply. The signalman is silhouetted in his box, controlling one crossover, one long siding and associated signals.

Plate 75: **Eythorne** was the first station out of Shepherd's Well on the East Kent Railway. It closed in 1948. Eleven years later, the shelter has disappeared, but the platform remains, edged with what look like old sleepers. It mainly served the mining community – a few modern houses stand on the left. A winding wheel of Tilmanstone colliery can be seen in the distance. New concrete-sleeper track has been laid for the remaining coal traffic. Beyond the ungated road crossing, coal trains branch to the right at 10 mph, together with the 4-wire telegraph. Passenger and general goods trains would once have gone straight ahead on a track now lifted.

Plate 77 (*opposite*): **Loughborough Junction** was three-directional with six platforms. One can imagine scenes, in the Jacques Tati tradition, of passengers rushing in hordes between platforms, seeking the next train to Ludgate Hill. This is the Cambria Road spur whose platforms closed in 1925. The elevated Down platform is severely curved and narrow, with a modest waiting room and canopy. A concrete cable duct is laid along its length, presumably for telegraph lines. Semaphore signalling remained in use until 1963. Note the twenty-six chimney pots on the adjacent houses – air pollution must once have been heavy for passengers waiting here in the fog.

Plate 76: **Tovil** station, to the south-east of Maidstone, opened in 1883 and closed in 1943. All that remained in 1961 were two grassy banks and a footbridge. The telegraph connection to the right was presumably a public supply line. One prospective passenger awaits an imaginary stopping train to Paddock Wood.

Plate 78 (*opposite, above*): **Ramsgate Harbour** was a compact terminus, romantically located on the beach with a spectacular tunnel approach, whose angled portal is seen here on the right. Opened by the LCDR in 1863, it was closed in 1926 as part of the Southern's rationalisation of Thanet and become a fairground. Photographed in 1959, *Merrie England* has replaced the arched roof over the two main platforms which had a turntable beyond. A small storage/loco yard was tucked beyond the helter-skelter, while three carriage sidings passed beneath the camera position. It was a gallant contribution to promoting holiday and excursion traffic from London. The harbour arm can be seen in the distance and shellfish are sold by the pint at the stalls on the left.

Plate 80 (*above*): Below the White Cliffs is the site of **Dover Harbour** station, with the former LCDR buildings and tower on the left. It once had an overall triangular roof covering two through-lines. The junction leads to Dover Marine (right) and to the SER main line via the Hawkesbury Street curve (foreground). The original alignment of this curve was along the siding where the SNCF van stands. Other items of interest include the 'cats-eye' Whistle sign, several lattice footbridges, a fogman's hut and a smart SR signal bracket. The short, circled semaphore is for entry into the Western Docks (far right). As with all Victorian dock areas, the railway was dominant. The LCDR main line runs straight ahead through the tunnel to Dover Priory station.

Plate 79 (*opposite, below*): The LCDR's **Dover Harbour** station opened in 1861 and closed in 1927, superseded by the SECR's Dover Marine. Forty-two years after closure, the former booking office looks in remarkably good condition. Although the doors and windows are mostly bricked up or barred, the splendour of fine brickwork and shapely arches can still be appreciated in the four pavilions. The associated tower once had a roofed turret resembling a lighthouse. It was a short walk to the cross-channel packets moored at Admiralty Pier. They would have been tidal packets originally, with boat trains running at different times each day.

Plate 81: **Tilmanstone** colliery was served by the independent East Kent Railway, which opened in 1912, engineered and managed by Colonel Stephens. It had a chequered history, carrying coals via Shepherd's Well and for a short while via Richborough Port. Although nationalised into BR(S) in 1948, the EKR was immediately abandoned, except for a couple of miles to Tilmanstone colliery (see *plate 100*). Eleven years later, the track was still in place, but Tilmanstone's passenger platform is heavily disguised with grass. The brick platform is substantial, but devoid of facilities. It represents a sad end to this romantic little railway.

Plate 82: **Wootton** station opened in 1875 and closed in 1953. Road-bridge arches accommodated both the platform end (seen here) and the booking office (to the right). Seven years after closure, the approach ramp and platform are grassed over. The IOWCR favoured concrete edging cast *in situ*, seen here in the foreground. One section of platform has been dismantled, probably because of earth slippage. A new station was opened here in 1986, just short of the bridge (behind the camera), as the western terminus of the Isle of Wight Steam Railway.

Plate 83: After the First World War, the East Kent Railway was extended through Eastry northwards to Richborough, with a branch eastwards to Wingham. These lines were uneconomic but picturesque, combining beautiful scenery with quaint, archaic trains. This former road crossing, a mile north of **Tilmanstone**, shows the steep incline of the old line and the intimacy of the railway with the countryside. The cast-iron, pre-war road sign stands out vividly against the Kentish fields and winter trees.

Plate 84: **Biddenden** station opened in 1905, part of the northern extension of the Kent & East Sussex Railway (another little line managed by Colonel Stephens). Nationalised in 1948 into BR(S), the northern section closed in 1954. Seven years later, the track-bed and platform are covered in grass and saplings, but the simple wooden building still looks serviceable. The backward-sloping canopy with wooden posts and 45° props are characteristic of K&ESR, so too the corrugated metal roof. Steam can still be enjoyed on the preserved southern section of this line between Tenterden, Rolvenden, Northiam and Bodiam – LBSCR 'Terrier' tanks are a speciality.

Plate 85: The Newport, Godshill & St Lawrence Railway was over-optimistic about traffic when its line to Ventnor West was built. Instead of 'making do' with a halt, **St Lawrence** was provided with a substantial two-storey station building where the stationman lived. Opened in 1897 and closed in 1953, it had a single platform and no siding. The station is enclosed by a winding road, steeply rising to the bridge at the Ventnor end. On a model railway, such a disposition would make a fine entry into hidden sidings. The fence, platform and track-bed look neglected, seven years after closure. The building looks more like a pub.

Plate 86: The main platform at **Ventnor West**, viewed from the buffer stops. There was once a cantilevered canopy along the central section of the building and a second platform on the right (with no building). There were sidings at the far end for goods and loco servicing. The platform end has been cut away to facilitate lorry access, presumably for line dismantling. Large blocks of reusable stone adorn the platform. (See also *plate 21*).

Plate 87: **Merstone** is a sad sight. Once a junction station for Ventnor West, it closed in 1956 to become grass-infested with nearly every window broken. The island platform has a gabled, single-storey brick building, with passenger access from the level-crossing (see *plate 162*). Its dominant features are the great cantilevered canopy and the thoughtful end partitions whose multiple window panes are in the LSWR tradition (*plate 58*). However, the valance has more in common with the SER. Despite these comforts and frills, this was a bleak, remote site.

Plate 88: St Helens station building is a smaller version of Bembridge (see *plate 20*) – an ornate, two-storey, gabled block with great Tudor-style chimneys, but marred by a huge wooden canopy along the platform. The building date of 1877 is clear, although the branch did not open until 1882. It closed in 1953 and still looks in good condition, seven years later. The white banding on the canopy posts is a relic from the wartime blackout.

5 Yards, Sheds and Huts

Local goods yards were mostly spacious, with generous length, width and height allowed for road carts, open docks, covered docks (goods sheds), warehouses and coal storage staithes. They were designed for peak traffic (often seasonal) which declined during the twentieth century as lorries and vans stole their business. Local goods yards became grossly under-utilised during the BR era. Only coal survived as a major rail commodity, yielding to natural gas during the late 1960s and early 1970s as the main domestic and commercial fuel.

Goods yards are remembered as an integral part of local stations during the heyday of steam. It was enthralling to watch an 0–6–0 steam locomotive shunting in the yard. Several engines are captured in the yards in this chapter, although most of the pictures show local yards as they really were for most of the time – in suspended animation. A few works and locomotive yards are included showing more intensive activity. Finally, there are three assorted platelayers' huts and one industrial yard tucked between railway viaducts.

Plate 89: This goods yard at **Mayfield** has a bay, a siding through the goods shed, one general siding and one long siding with coal staithes. The site is beautifully laid out on a curve, with a substantial LBSCR station building. Built on a hillside, the site has been levelled, in contrast to the SER station at Wadhurst (opposite).

Plate 90: **Wadhurst** station is built on a hillside with unusual three-level terracing for the yards and roads. On the top level is the general goods yard, comprising a single siding, brick shed, crane and vehicle parking spaces. On the middle level is the coal siding with staithes, with a small lamp guarding the ungated crossing. At the bottom level (right) is the passenger approach road with what looks like a Dinky car. The Italianate station building is substantial. From the far, wooded hillside, the white fence of a footpath leads directly to the footbridge.

Plate 91: The goods yard at **Bat & Ball** diverges from the running lines to make a Y-shape, with the station forecourt in between and a signal box guarding the throat. The station building and goods shed are from a late phase of LCDR architecture – well proportioned and nicely finished in coloured brickwork with some ornate arches and eaves. The long canopy, with plain, slotted valancing, is most welcoming, as is the door to the stationmaster's two-storey house. Coal is the principal commodity in the yard, the shed is disused.

Plate 92: **Hawkhurst** had a small, simple goods shed, but with some delightful multi-coloured brickwork, enhanced by encroaching grass and wild flowers. Part of the roof is glazed and there is a circular window at either end. Despite a busy appearance, the vehicle entrances are locked. The SR vans are simply stored there.

Plate 93: **Littlehampton** has one exceptionally long island platform to accommodate 12-car EMUs from London. It is studded with concrete SR art-deco lamp standards, which resemble medieval religious banners with their loudspeakers, hanging lamp shades, top insulators and an unusual trophy-like finial. The LBSCR goods shed is much older, but is also exceptional, having two storeys with fine brickwork and top lights.

Plate 94: The goods yard at **Wadebridge** was on the Down side. It included a cattle pen and a goods shed – nicely finished in local stone with a square end-window. It is attended here by Beattie well-tank No. 30587 with a GWR 'toad' brake van. Engine shed vents and a water tower can be seen on the Up side where GWR Prairie tank No. 4565 prepares to take a short passenger train to Bodmin General. The GWR and the LSWR/SR co-existed here amicably for some eight decades, but the tiny LSWR well-tanks usually stole the show.

Plate 95: A staggered platform and the goods yard at **Chilham**. The SER shed proportions are similar to Bat & Ball's, but less ornate, with lintels instead of arches. At least it still has general goods. Bulleid 0–6–0 class Q1 No. 33015 is signalled through with the pick-up goods to Canterbury West, running bunker first with wooden open wagons. The S&F Type 12a signal box is identified by its gabled roof with a pronounced overhang.

Plate 96: A functional, stone-built goods shed at **Shepton Mallet Charlton Road**, with the office tacked on one end. The loading gauge is SR concrete. There is a tall yard lamp opposite, by a water column, which is lagged and encased in wood, with a great brazier alongside. There are goods sidings to either side of the running lines – coal can be seen on the right. A north-bound train approaches, headed by a standard class 5MT.

Plate 97: The goods sheds at **Hellingly** are unusual, being more akin to American railways. The large, open shed has no platform and looks disused, holding two empty wagons – a 2-plank and a bogie flat. The storage shed beyond is large and multi-storey, cheaply clad in corrugated metal upon a brick base. The goods yard as a whole seems disproportionately large for such a remote, rural location. There is a covered wagon by the station building, but only the coal siding looks busy, with two modest piles of coal and one steel wagon.

Plate 98: The water tower at **Faversham** was located on a separate site from the MPD and associated yards. It is a substantial brick structure with some ornate, round-headed windows, doors and recesses. The steel tank is shallow and supports a corrugated roof with railings. The purpose of the foreground winch is uncertain.

Plate 99: A hemmed-in goods siding in the old yard at **Callington**, between goods offices on the left and a coal-drop on the right. A number of the buildings here pre-dated the railway.

Plate 101: A busy scene at **Fratton MPD**, with a one point lever and five parallel roads for locomotive servicing. Left to right, the line functions are: watering; ashing; coaling; coal cranage and coal wagon storage. The first three all have ash pits, entered via the three-way point from the engine shed behind the camera. Two standard class 4s are nearest the camera. Their fountain domes are prominent but useless appendages, since there are no water troughs on the Southern. Wagons are an interesting mix of steel, 5-plank and 7-plank wooden variations.

Plate 100 (*opposite, below*): The existence of the Kent coalfield was confirmed in 1890 during trial borings at Dover for the Channel Tunnel. Many pits were dug in the Dover–Sandwich–Canterbury triangle, of which **Tilmanstone** was the most successful. Surface workings are more extensive than their village namesake, about a mile away. In this satanic landscape, worthy of Charles Dickens' *Hard Times*, three winding wheels are visible, together with washeries, a power house chimney and a long, low slag heap. The serpentine sidings hold BR steel mineral wagons, as well as a few older wooden ones (see *plate 81* for the former passenger platform nearby).

Plate 102: Skewed bridges and a sunken goods yard at **New Cross Gate**, with three long sidings packed with coal wagons. The steep incline leads to the LBSCR main line and New Cross Gate station. The embankment to the right leads to junctions for the South London line, the East London line and the Deptford Wharf branch.

Plate 103: **Ryde St John's Road** was the engineering base of the Isle of Wight Railway. During the 1920s, the SR built a new (larger) MPD on the Up side, seen here to the left of the signal box and comprising two coaling roads, two shed roads and storage sidings. The yard on the Down side then became just the Works. The old (black) engine shed can be seen on the far right. Next to it is the brick-built workshop for locomotive repairs and maintenance (see *plate 232*). Adjacent to the island platform is the Carriage & Wagon workshop, rebuilt during the late 1930s. Note the tall SR yard lamps, the trunk telegraph, point lever and shunting signal. This quiet scene is deceptive – for most of the day it was alive with passenger trains and locomotive movements.

Plate 104: The goods yard at **Forest Row** was entered via a siding on the Up side, alongside the S&F Type 5 signal box. A train of redundant BR steam stock is stored on the longest siding, awaiting its fate, shortly after dieselisation in 1963. The brick goods shed looks disused; indeed, the only remaining freight is coal, seen heaped by the passenger approach road in *plate 11*. There is a farm gate (left) with a little-used crossing over the siding points. The enamel on the Westinghouse shunting disc is damaged with a prominent streak of rust.

Plate 105: **Newport** was the engineering base of the Isle of Wight Central Railway. It also boasted the island's largest station and the most extensive yards, seen here from storage sidings by the Cowes line. Closure started in 1953 with the Freshwater branch, seen curving to the right beyond the signal box. The latter is of RSCo design (see *plate 162*). The SR signal bracket has an exceptionally long cantilevered platform. A class O2 tank shunts mineral wagons in the Freshwater goods yard. The engine shed, bereft of its clerestory, stands between the station and the water tower (left), relegated in 1957 to crane storage. The Works behind the grounded coach bodies (left) only handled carriage painting from 1957. Everything closed in 1966; it was the end of an empire.

Plate 106: **Sturminster Newton** from the south, showing (from left) the LSWR Type 1 signal box, the passenger station and a classic country goods yard, fanning out to the right and entered via a double-slip point. The brick goods shed looks little-used, but there is one coal wagon and three sidings full of vans. The style of platform canopy tells us that this is an S&D location. See *plate 61* for a view from the far end by the bridge.

Plate 109: An abandoned platelayers' hut on the Ventnor West branch near **Whitwell**. The vertical panelling is similar to Brasted's, but the roof has a greater pitch. The door remains locked, but undergrowth is encroaching, the chimney is toppling and a hole has appeared above the door, perfect access for blackbirds.

Plate 107 (*opposite above*): A delightful platelayers' hut at **Brasted**, with vertical panelling, a felt roof and a brick chimney with a tall pot. A bridge gauge is strapped to the front. The carpenter's sawhorse is for sawing sleepers.

Plate 108 (*opposite, below*): An urban panorama looking east from **Shepherd's Lane** signal box. The LCDR main line is on the left while the LBSCR's South London Line rises on a reverse curve to the right. In between is an industrial yard with lorries, sheds and a square brick chimney. Such pokey yards were commonplace between railway viaducts. Largely hidden from the public gaze, they make interesting fill-ins for model railways.

Plate 110 (*below*): A newly built platelayers' hut near **North Hayling**, made of old sleepers, butted together vertically. Not quite finished, it was no doubt awaiting proper doors, a window and a chimneystack or stovepipe.

6 Railway Ephemera and Signs

Railway ephemera are printed pieces of paper and card intended for a short life. Included here are a Kent Coast Electrification leaflet, a leaflet on Ashford Works, an SR *Luggage in Advance* form, a selection of SR and BR tickets (arranged geographically), two historic letters from the S&D and SECR, and some SR and BR Season and Holiday Runabout tickets. They are followed by a selection of signs in metal, concrete, wood and stone, as well as a few posters. Collectively, they are a reminder of the tremendous clerical support and office skills needed to keep a railway running. Accountants, PR officers, sales & marketing people, traffic planners, designers, printers and booking clerks were as essential to smooth running as train crews, signalmen and platelayers. It was a team effort.

By modern standards, much of this collection looks antiquated in style and content. The flowery nib-and-ink scrawl of the SECR letter is barely legible, while the typed S&D circular of 1921 is excruciatingly detailed. The third page of the Luggage in Advance form makes fascinating reading regarding the list of applicable items – they include Alpenstocks, Schoolboys' Tuck Boxes, Deck Chairs (folded) and Gun Cases containing Sporting Guns. Waterloo Station would be cleared if guns were found today. The tickets too are historical both for their form (just over 2in x 1in card) and for their stations, most of which are now closed. The Isle of Wight was particularly rich in old tickets. Finally, please refer also to the SR double-sided folding map of 1929 which is reproduced at the front as *plate 2*.

Plate 111 (*below*): An extract from a BR(S) Modernisation leaflet of 1958: *Transforming the Railway in the South-East.* The steam locomotive is SECR 4–4–0 class D1 No. 31749, built in 1903 at the Vulcan Foundry.

You can sum up the whole modernisation scheme for Kent by saying—we are getting rid of steam as quickly as possible.

Steam locomotives are romantic, impressive, and have a proud history as the great work-horses of industrial Britain.

When travel problems were simpler they did the job superbly. But steam loco-motion just cannot cope with the tasks of a railway network which needs to run on split minutes to move people about on a scale never before attempted.

For this sort of intensive transport, steam trains are too cumbersome. The termini, for instance, can handle far fewer steam trains since it takes so much longer to turn them round than it does electric or diesel-electric trains. More serious, however, is the fact that they are too unpredictable in their behaviour, and too vulnerable to all sorts of upsets.

Even a handful of them operating on a partly electrified system can throw everything else out of gear—and as you probably know too well, often do.

A large part of the Kent lines is already electrified. Our plan is to change over completely to either electric or diesel-electric trains on all the remaining lines.

Electrification involves huge engineering jobs and cannot be done overnight. And, as we have pointed out, to do the work reasonably quickly must interfere with existing train services.

But you may find your train affected by work connected with electrifying somebody else's route. That seems infuriatingly unfair. But the real point is that every steam train that we can get rid of on the system benefits the running of all trains—even, for the time being, the remaining steam trains.

HOW WE AR

AT'S BEING DONE?

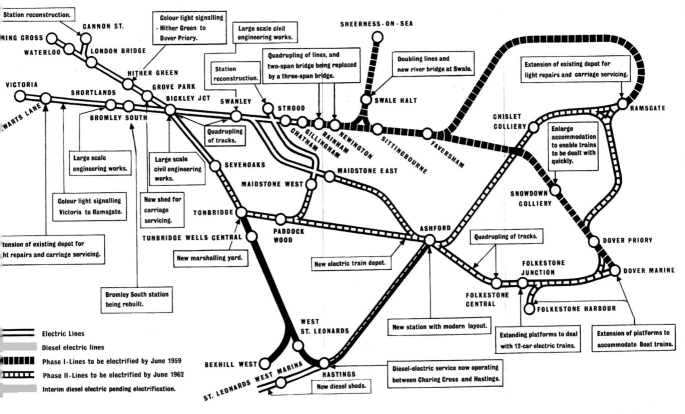

Station reconstruction.

CANNON ST.

Colour light signalling - Hither Green to Dover Priory.

Large scale civil engineering works.

SHEERNESS-ON-SEA

RING CROSS

WATERLOO

LONDON BRIDGE

Quadrupling of lines, and two-span bridge being replaced by a three-span bridge.

Doubling lines and new river bridge at Swale.

Extension of existing depot for light repairs and carriage servicing.

HITHER GREEN

Station reconstruction.

GROVE PARK

SWALE HALT

RAMSGATE

VICTORIA

SHORTLANDS

BICKLEY JCT

SWANLEY

STROOD

CHISLET COLLIERY

WARTS LANE

BROMLEY SOUTH

Quadrupling of tracks.

GILLINGHAM

CHATHAM

RAINHAM

NEWINGTON

SITTINGBOURNE

FAVERSHAM

Enlarge accommodation to enable trains to be dealt with quickly.

Large scale engineering works.

Large scale civil engineering works.

SEVENOAKS

MAIDSTONE EAST

SNOWDOWN COLLIERY

Colour light signalling Victoria to Ramsgate.

New shed for carriage servicing.

MAIDSTONE WEST

TONBRIDGE

DOVER PRIORY

Extension of existing depot for light repairs and carriage servicing.

TUNBRIDGE WELLS CENTRAL

PADDOCK WOOD

ASHFORD

Quadrupling of tracks.

FOLKESTONE JUNCTION

DOVER MARINE

FOLKESTONE CENTRAL

FOLKESTONE HARBOUR

New marshalling yard.

New electric train depot.

Bromley South station being rebuilt.

WEST ST. LEONARDS

New station with modern layout.

Extending platforms to deal with 12-car electric trains.

Extension of platforms to accommodate Boat trains.

BEXHILL WEST

ST. LEONARDS WEST MARINA

HASTINGS

Diesel-electric service now operating between Charing Cross and Hastings.

New diesel sheds.

Electric Lines

Diesel electric lines

Phase I-Lines to be electrified by June 1959

Phase II-Lines to be electrified by June 1962

Interim diesel electric pending electrification.

Plate 112: A further extract from the same leaflet of 1958. Phase II lines were in fact electrified in 1961, but the Ashford to Hastings line was not electrified and Folkestone was quadrupled only as far as Cheriton.

Plate 113: The descriptive pages of Ashford Locomotive Works, from a BR(S) leaflet.

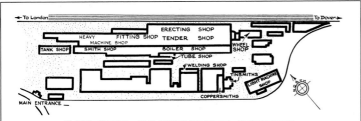

ASHFORD LOCOMOTIVE WORKS

It was in February of the Year 1846 that the Board of Directors of the South Eastern Railway decided to purchase 185 acres of good Kentish countryside on which to lay the foundations of a "Locomotive Establishment".

In the summer of 1847, in the shape of a cluster of 72 Labourers' cottages, there arose the first signs of a new Railway project and the story of Ashford Works had begun. Towards the end of the same year, the inaugural meeting of the Ashford Works Mechanics' Institute took place at which the Chairman of the Board stressed that the construction work was not merely of a fine and well equipped Locomotive Works but of a complete village. In the autumn of the same year official news was given that the Railway's Locomotive Depot at New Cross would be transferred to the new site at Ashford.

In the Year 1848 work had begun on the first new locomotive to be built at the Works.

In the autumn of 1850 the creation of the Carriage and Wagon Works was seen at Ashford. By this time the adjoining Railway village, known at first by the name of Alfred Town, had been expanded by another 60 houses and the Gas Works was making an appearance on the site.

When the old Railway Companies were grouped in 1923, Ashford became one of the three main Works of the Southern Railway and dealt with the construction and repair of locomotives, carriages and wagons.

The construction of new coaches was transferred to Eastleigh and, in the main, carriage repairs to Lancing in the Year 1929, and since then the main activity of the Carriage and Wagon Works has been the building and repair of wagon stock.

Nationalisation in 1948 eventually placed the Locomotive Works under the jurisdiction of the Mechanical and Electrical Engineer and occupies an area of 26½ acres, and the Carriage and Wagon Works under the Carriage and Wagon Engineer occupying some 40 acres, the combined total area being 66½ acres.

The Locomotive Works is at present mainly engaged in the repair of locomotives, together with the manufacture of details for new locomotives erected at Brighton and elsewhere, one of the last new locomotives constructed at this Works being the Main Line Diesel Electric Locomotive No. 10202 released in the autumn of 1951.

Visitors to the Works will see many machines of modern design and up-to-date methods of production.

Heavy Machine Shop
The Machine section manufactures parts for locomotives from castings and forgings. Up-to-date machinery is installed for planing, slotting, shaping, drilling, centre lathe turning.
Flame cutting of main frames for standard locomotives is also carried out in this Shop.

Light Machine Shop
The equipment of this Shop in the main is made up of Capstan and Turret Lathes but also includes 6-Spindle, 4-Spindle and single Spindle, Automatic Machines. Production includes turned bolts, pins, firebox stays, union nuts, pipe cones, collars.

Tool Room
Jigs, gauges and precision tools are made in this Shop, which is equipped with lathes, milling, grinding and other machines. A Comparator is also available for measuring to very fine limits.

Fitting Shop
The fitting of valve gear, coupling and connecting rods, sanding gear, brake gear and cylinders is carried out in this Shop.

Erecting Shop
This shop is equipped with five overhead cranes, two capable of lifting 50 Tons each, one 35 Tons and two 30 Tons. Locomotives are stripped, the parts being cleaned in the "Bosh" and sent to various shops for repair.
A progressive system of erection is adopted, the frames being repaired, including the fitting of frame inserts, and set to a "datum" system, ensuring they are correctly aligned.
Maximum use is made of portable grinding, drilling, flame-cutting, machining and electric welding sets.

Boiler Shop
This Shop is served by two 25 Ton and one 10 Ton overhead travelling cranes to facilitate the movement and repair of locomotive boilers. Other equipment consists of plate levelling rolls, plate edge planer, radial drilling machines and 200 Ton hydraulic flanging press.
A Hi-Cycle plant operating at 125 Volts, 200 Cycles, 3-Phase, is used for the drilling and tapping of fireboxes.
Maximum use is made of Hi-Cycle power and compressed air for portable grinding and drilling machines.

Tube Shop
In this Shop is undertaken the de-scaling and re-conditioning of about 1,500 small boiler tubes per week. The lay-out is progressive and includes the butt welding of new ends to old tubes.

Smiths Shop
This Shop is equipped with electro pneumatic hammers and deals with all the work for repairs and some new building details. An electric butt welder is used in the manufacture of spring buckles, brake rods and other components.

Wheel Shop
The re-tyring of wheels and re-turning of tyres and journals and other necessary work in connection with the repair of wheels are carried out in this Shop.

Coppersmiths Shop
The repair of all copper pipes for locomotive and the repair and testing of superheater flue tubes and elements is carried out here.

Sheet Metal Shop
The manufacture and repair of lamps, oil feeders, torch lamps and other sheet metal work, much of which is of welded construction, is undertaken in this Shop.

Whitemetal Shop
In this Shop is carried out the manufacture and re-conditioning of whitemetal and the manufacture of solder for the Southern Region and the filling of bearings.

Welding Shop
The fabrication of components and the re-clamation of worn parts is executed in this Shop. Both electric and oxy-acetylene welding is employed.

AD 6921/A5   Printed in Great Britain by A. White & Co. Ltd., London, E.15.

SOUTHERN RAILWAY

→ **These facilities apply ONLY to RAIL Passengers. Owners of luggage NOT travelling by RAIL will be required to pay the ordinary charges applicable.**

$\left(\dfrac{\text{Stock}}{1611\ \text{C}}\right)$
6/41

PASSENGERS' LUGGAGE
COLLECTED, CONVEYED
AND
DELIVERED
IN ADVANCE

IMPORTANT.

FILL IN THIS CONSIGNMENT NOTE
and
SEND IT TO THE STATION
or
HAND IT TO THE CARMAN.

RAILWAY TICKET(S) MUST BE PRODUCED BEFORE LUGGAGE CAN BE ACCEPTED.

When collection is required ("P.L.A." or "C.L."), this Consignment Note, after being filled in, should be handed to the Carman, or sent to the appropriate Station so as to be received by the Company twenty-four hours before the collection is desired to be made.

LONDON.

For Collection from addresses within the following Postal Districts, viz :—

E.C. 1, 2, 3, 4.	N.W. 1, 8.	E. 1, 2.	N. 1.
W.C. 1, 2.	S.W. 1, 3, 5, 7, 10.	W. 1, 2, 8, 9, 11.	S.E. 1, 11, 17.

the Consignment Note should be handed in at, or addressed to, the **Parcels Office** at :—

WATERLOO STATION, S.E.1.

Orders for Collection within other London Postal Districts, also London Suburbs, should be handed in at, or addressed to, the nearest Station to Owner's address.

COUNTRY AND SEASIDE.

Orders for Collection should be handed in at, or addressed to, the Station from which the Passenger's journey will commence.

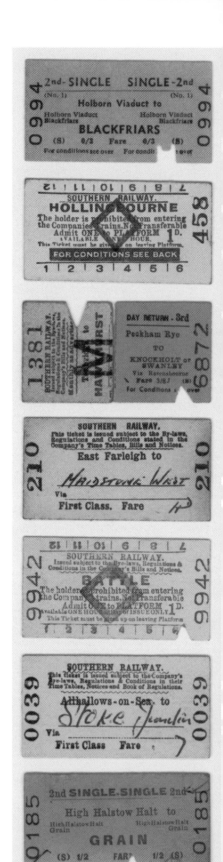

Plate 114 (*above and on the next three pages*): A four-page SR form from 1941 for Passengers' Luggage in Advance.

2nd- SINGLE   SINGLE -2nd
New Cross Gate to
New Cross Gate · Brighton or Hove
BRIGHTON or HOVE
via East Croydon
(S) 12/0   Fare   12/0 (S)
For conditions see over   For conditions see over
4958   4958

BRITISH RAILWAYS (S)
UPPER WARLINGHAM
PLATFORM TICKET 1d.
Available ONE HOUR on Day of issue only
NOT VALID IN TRAINS. NOT TRANSFERABLE
To be given up when leaving Platform.
FOR CONDITIONS SEE BACK
9402   9402
1   2   3   4   5   6

SOUTHERN RAILWAY.
Issued subject to the Bye-laws, Regulations &
Conditions in the Co's Time Tables, Bills & Notices.
Ockley & Capel to
Holmwood
Via
First Class. Fare 1/2
NOT TRANSFERABLE
0523   0523

SOUTHERN RAILWAY
BRAMLEY & WONERSH
Adult 1d
This ... ... up on
leaving
Available ONE HOUR Not transferable
FOR CONDITIONS SEE BACK.
0647   0647
1   2   3   4   5   6

SOUTHERN RAILWAY.
Slinfold   Baynards
Slinfold to
Slinfold   Baynards
BAYNARDS
THIRD CLASS   THIRD CLASS
Fare 6d.   Fare 6d.
FOR CONDITIONS SEE BACK
0398   0398

SOUTHERN RAILWAY.
Issued subject to the Bye-laws, Regulations &
Conditions in the Company's Bills and Notices.
Southwater to
WEST GRINSTEAD
Via
First Class Fare -/-
NOT TRANSFERABLE.
0123   0123

SOUTHERN RAILWAY.
Issued subject to the Bye-laws, Regulations &
Conditions in the Company's Bills and Notices.
Langston   Langston
Langston to
North Hayling   North Hayling
NORTH HAYLING
THIRD CLASS   THIRD CLASS
Fare 2½d.   Fare 2½d.
NOT TRANSFERABLE
3618   3618

---

(2)

LUGGAGE IN ADVANCE
CONSIGNMENT NOTE

(This arrangement is ~~not applicable~~ to the Luggage of Holders of Day or Half-Day Tickets issued at less than the ordinary fare).

TO THE SOUTHERN RAILWAY COMPANY.

Please*collect / accept

....
(Number and description of packages and/or articles).

from..

....
(Full forwarding Address †).

on..for conveyance to :—
(Date.)

....
(Owner's Name.)

....

....
(Full destination Address †.)

....
(Destination Station or Port and Railway Co.)

I, *hold / will obtain..ticket(s) as follows, and

will produce *it / them on demand :—

Number of Tickets.	Class.	Description (Ordinary, Tourist, Monthly, etc.)	Stations.		For Official Use.	
			From.	To.	Number(s) on Ticket(s).	Inspected by.
...... Adult						
...... Child						

I declare that the Luggage or other article will be strictly in accordance with the permitted descriptions specified in Condition (C) (i) & (ii) on page 3 hereof, and that it is the property of the holder(s) of the above-mentioned ticket(s).

If there is not a through booking to the Destination Station or Port to which the Luggage or other article is to be conveyed, I undertake to purchase the further Railway or Steamship Ticket(s) necessary to complete the journey to such Destination.

In consideration of your accepting the Luggage or other article at the Reduced Charge, I agree to be bound by the Conditions shown in this Consignment Note and in the Company's Time Tables, Notices, and/or Book of General Regulations relating to Traffic by Passenger Train or other similar service.

Signature..

Permanent Address..

These facilities apply ONLY to RAIL Passengers. Owners of luggage NOT travelling by RAIL will be required to pay the ordinary charges applicable.

....

Date..19......

*Strike out words not applicable.
† If the address is in London, please include Postal District Number.

Plate 115 (*above and on the next three pages*): A selection of old and interesting tickets from the SR and BR.

CONDITIONS.

(A) REQUIREMENTS TO BE COMPLIED WITH BY OWNER.

1. Travel by Railway to the Destination Station or Port, and produce Railway Ticket(s) before the Luggage is handed to the Company.

2. Securely affix a label, or labels, to each package, clearly indicating (1) the Owner's full name and address, also the Destination Station or Port, or (2) the Owner's name and the name of the Destination Station or Port, in the case of Luggage "To be called for."

3. **Enclose duplicate address label in each package.**

4. Efficiently secure all packages, and strap or cord trunks and boxes.

5. **Remove or obliterate all old labels or addresses.**

(B) STATIONS BETWEEN WHICH THE ARRANGEMENTS OPERATE.

Between all Southern Railway Stations (including Stations in the Isle of Wight).

Between Southern Railway Stations, as above, and Stations on other Railways in Great Britain (other than on the London Passenger Transport Board) including the Isle of Man.

(C) LUGGAGE TO WHICH APPLICABLE.

(i) The arrangements apply only to packages and articles of the following description, viz. :—Portmanteaux, Bags, Trunks, Dress Baskets, Suit Cases, Boxes, etc., containing the **Passenger's personal luggage only,** also Cricket Bags and Golf Clubs properly secured, Skis, Alpenstocks, Schoolboys' Tuck Boxes, Gun Cases containing Sporting Guns, Fishing Rods in wooden cases, Deck Chairs (folded), Play-pens (folded), Camp Equipment such as small tents (folded), and poles, and Commercial Travellers' Luggage.

BUT NOT TO ARTICLES SUCH AS:

Bedding, Furniture or Merchandise (packed or not packed), Cameras and Camera Stands, Gramophones, Lecturers Apparatus (including lantern), Motor Cycles (including fore-carriages or trailers), Sewing Machines, Wireless Sets. Tool Boxes belonging to Craftsmen, Musical Instruments.

(ii) A Passenger's Cycle (not Motor), Perambulator (not folded, empty), Mail Cart (not folded, empty), Bath Chair (empty), Tricycle (not motor), Invalid Chair (not folded, empty), may also be forwarded in advance, and will be charged at the same rate as though the article accompanied the Passenger, plus the fee for "P.L.A.," "C.L.," or "D.L." A Perambulator loaded with personal luggage sent under these Arrangements will be charged the ordinary scale rate applicable to Perambulators (not folded) accompanying Passengers, plus the "P.L.A.," "C.L.," or "D.L." fee, and if the total weight, after deducting an allowance of 60 lbs. for the weight of the Perambulator, exceeds the authorised free allowance, the excess weight will be charged for at the ordinary Excess Luggage Rate.

A Perambulator (folded, empty), Mail Cart (folded, empty), SMALL Invalid Chair (folded, empty), or Child's Cot (folded, empty), will be charged only the "P.L.A.," "C.L." or "D.L." fee.

(iii) The Company will not undertake to carry or convey under these arrangements packages of Luggage containing Jewellery, Bullion, Coins, Bank or Treasury Notes, Trinkets, Precious Stones, Cameras, Field Glasses, or other valuable articles of a similar character, whether or not exceeding £25 in value and the Company will under no circumstances be liable for the loss of or injury or damage to any of the articles or things named.

MATCHES or other goods of a dangerous nature must *not* be enclosed in packages sent under these arrangements.

(D) CHARGES (which must be prepaid).

Collection, Conveyance and Delivery ("P.L.A.") ...	2s. 4d. per package	Subject
Conveyance and Delivery ("D.L.")	1s. 2d. „	to
*Conveyance, or Collection & Conveyance ("C.L.")...	1s. 2d. „	clauses (E)

except to and from the Isle of Man, in which case the Charges will be increased by 7d. In the **(F) and (H)** Isle of Man cartage facilities are provided at Douglas only.

*Only applicable to Luggage and articles addressed "To be called for" at the Destination Station or Port.

The Charges include Collection from and/or Delivery to addresses within the recognised free radius at Stations or Ports where Cartage Services are in operation.

Two packages or articles tied together will be charged separately.

(E) CARTAGE ARRANGEMENTS.

The Service of Collection or Delivery does not include the carrying of Luggage from or to the upper rooms of buildings, or from or to basements.

No Cartage Services are in operation on Sundays, Christmas Day, Good Friday, Bank Holidays or other Public Holidays, nor will the Company undertake to collect or deliver outside the ordinary cartage hours.

Where Collection or Delivery is performed beyond the usual free Cartage area an additional Charge will be made.

(*Conditions continued on page 4*).

SOUTHERN RAILWAY.

....Station or Port

RECEIPT.

(*This must be surrendered when Luggage addressed "To be called for" is claimed at destination.*)

Received of...the sum of..............s...............d. for

(*Name*)

conveyance of.......................packages and/or articles of Passengers' Luggage in Advance

from.. to..

Date.............................19...... Signature...

(*For Extracts from Conditions, see back.*)

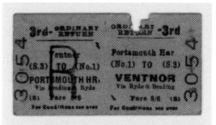

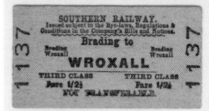

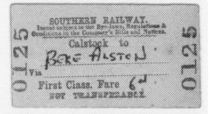

. (4)

CONDITIONS (continued from page 3.)

(F) WEIGHT OF LUGGAGE AND CHARGES FOR EXCESS WEIGHT.

Additional charges at the Excess Luggage Rate will be applicable when the total weight exceeds the usual Luggage allowance per Passenger viz. :—

1st Class Rail and/or Boat.	2nd Class Boat.	3rd Class Rail.	3rd Class Rail and 1st or 2nd Class Boat.
150 lbs.	120 lbs.	100 lbs.	100 lbs.

also in respect of any luggage accompanying the Passenger.

Passengers holding half-fare tickets are allowed one-half of the above weights.

Passengers should restrict the weight of each package to 112 lbs. to facilitate handling.

(G) LIABILITY.

The Company will not be liable for loss, damage or delay (a) of or to Luggage or Goods booked through for carriage partly by Railway and partly by water or wholly by water, arising from the Act of God, Act of War or of the King's enemies, fire, accidents from machinery, boilers and steam and all and every other dangers and accidents of the seas, rivers and navigation of whatever nature or kind. In respect of Luggage or Goods intended to be carried by Shipping Companies or other independent carrier the Company's obligations and liability notwithstanding that the Luggage or Goods may be addressed through to destination or may be carried at a through rate shall only relate or extend to that portion of the journey performed on the system of a Railway Company of Great Britain and the Company are authorised as agents for the Sender to contract for such carriage upon the terms of any Bill of Lading or other conditions usually required by such carrier ; (b) caused by or arising out of any strike, lock-out or riot or (c) resulting from any failure of the Owner to comply with any of the Conditions of this Consignment Note ; nor will they be liable for the loss of or injury to Furs and/or Lace which separately or in the aggregate exceed £25 in value unless at the time of forwarding the Owner shall declare the nature and value of such articles and pay an increased charge in respect of them.

No claim for damage or pilferage will be entertained unless made in writing within three days of the delivery of the luggage. In the case of non-delivery of a package no claim will be admitted unless complaint of loss is made in writing within 14 days of the date on which the package was handed to the Railway Company for despatch.

(H) STORAGE OF LUGGAGE.

Luggage remaining at the Railway Company's Destination Station or Port more than two days after arrival will be subject to the usual Cloak Room Conditions and Charges as exhibited at the Company's Stations and Offices. The Company will not be liable for loss, damage, misdelivery or detention however caused of or to any package or of or to any part thereof, if the total value of the package and its contents exceeds the sum of £5.

——FOLD HERE——

LUGGAGE IN ADVANCE.

To the PARCELS OFFICE,

SOUTHERN RAILWAY,

Station.

——FOLD HERE——

INSURANCE OF LUGGAGE.

Passengers can insure their Luggage under The Travellers' Baggage Insurance Association's arrangements. Insurance Tickets are obtainable at all Southern Railway Stations.

- - - - - - - - - - - - - - - - - - - -

EXTRACTS FROM CONDITIONS.

LIABILITY.

The Company will not be liable for loss, damage or delay (a) of or to Luggage or Goods booked through for carriage partly by Railway and partly by water or wholly by water, arising from the Act of God, Act of War or of the King's enemies, fire, accidents from machinery, boilers and steam and all and every other dangers and accidents of the seas, rivers and navigation of whatever nature or kind. In respect of Luggage or Goods intended to be carried by Shipping Companies or other independent carrier the Company's obligation and liability notwithstanding that the Luggage or Goods may be addressed through to destination or may be carried at a through rate shall only relate or extend to that portion of the journey performed on the system of a Railway Company of Great Britain and the Company are authorised as agents for the Sender to contract for such carriage upon the terms of any Bill of Lading or other conditions usually required by such carrier ; (b) caused by or arising out of any strike, lock-out or riot or (c) resulting from any failure of the Owner to comply with any of the Conditions of this Consignment Note ; nor will they be liable for the loss of or injury to Furs and/or Lace which separately or in the aggregate exceed £25 in value unless at the time of forwarding the Owner shall declare the nature and value of such articles and pay an increased charge in respect of them.

No claim for damage or pilferage will be entertained unless made in writing within three days of the delivery of the Luggage. In the case of non-delivery of a package no claim will be admitted unless complaint of loss is made in writing within 14 days of the date on which the package was handed to the Railway Company for despatch.

STORAGE OF LUGGAGE.

Luggage remaining at the Railway Company's Destination Station or Port more than two days after arrival will be subject to the usual Cloak Room Conditions and Charges as exhibited at the Company's Stations and Offices. The Company will not be liable for loss, damage, misdelivery or detention however caused of or to any package or of or to any part thereof, if the total value of the package and its contents exceeds the sum of £5.

(588A)
S. & D. F. 346A.
3721.

SOUTH WESTERN AND MIDLAND RAILWAY COMPANIES'

SOMERSET AND DORSET JOINT LINE.

Accountant's Office,

Circular C.9/89.

BATH.

18th October 1923

Railways Act, 1921.
Great Western Railway Group

I am now advised that, as from 1st November, 1923
the Station Accounts of the Midland and South Western Junction Company
will be amalgamated with those of the Great Western Company.

Traffic by Merchandise train, and Waybilled Parcel and
Miscellaneous traffic by Passenger train, with the above-named Company's
Stations should be returned in the same way as other Great Western traffic.

Passenger bookings from this Railway will be rendered to
the Clearing House separately from bookings at Great Western Stations proper,
and traffic in the reverse direction also should be returned separately to
this office.

Will you be good enough to issue the necessary instructions
to your Staff, and also arrange for traffic with the undermentioned places
(where there are duplicate Stations) to be specially indicated in the returns
in the manner shewn:-

Cirencester)		Swindon	G.W.
Marlborough)	G.W. or	Swindon Town	G.W.(M&SWJn.)
Savernake)	G.W.(M&SWJn)	∅ Cheltenham, St.James.	G.W.
Andoversford	G.W.	∅ Cheltenham, Malvern Rd.	G.W.
Andoversford &		∅ Cheltenham, Lansdown	G.W.(M&SWJn.)
Dowdeswell	G.W.(M&SWJn.)		
Burbage	G.W.	∅ Coaching traffic only affected	
Grafton &			
Burbage	G.W.(M&SWJn.)		

The following Stations of similar name should also be
specially distinguished, although they are situated in different localities:

Brill & Ludgershall	G.W.	Withington	G.W.
Ludgershall	G.W.(M&SWJn.)	Withington	G.W.(M&SWJn.)

A.R.Collier,

Accountant

Plate 116: An S&D accountant's circular, issued to station offices in 1923 and rescued from Shillingstone in 1963. It is a wonderful piece of bureaucracy about the impending grouping of the M&SWJR into the GWR and the need to differentiate respective stations of similar name. More tea, Sir Humphrey?

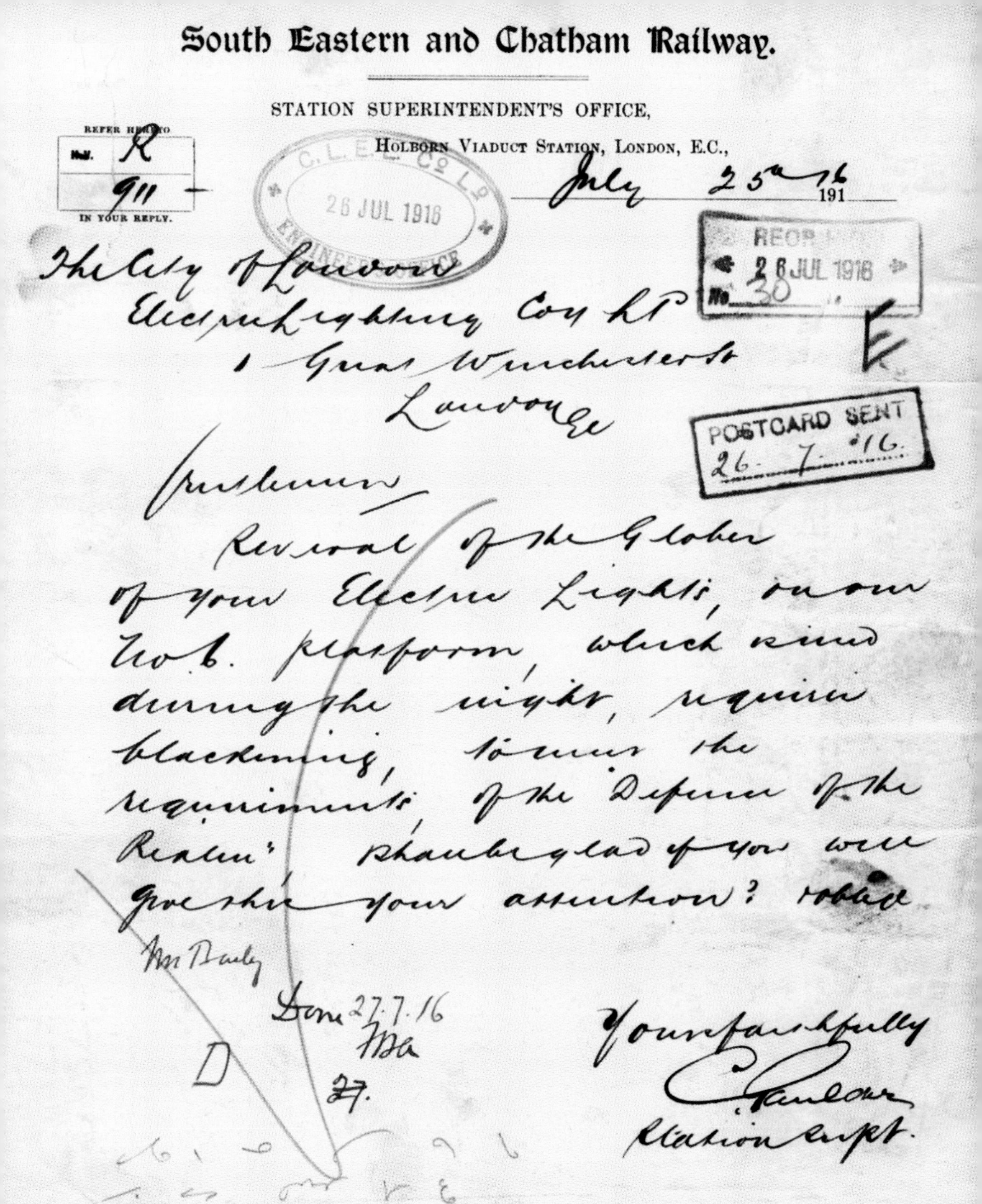

South Eastern and Chatham Railway.

STATION SUPERINTENDENT'S OFFICE,

HOLBORN VIADUCT STATION, LONDON, E.C.,

July 25ᵗʰ 16 191_

REFER HERETO
No. R
911 —
IN YOUR REPLY.

C.L.E.L. Co Ld
26 JUL 1916
ENGINEER'S OFFICE

REC'D
26 JUL 1916
No. 30

POSTCARD SENT
26. 7. '16.

The City of London
Electric Lighting Coy Ltd
1 Great Winchester St
London E.C.

Gentlemen,

Reversal of the Globes
of your Electric Lights, on our
No. 6. platform, which sind
during the night, require
blackening, to meet the
requirements of the "Defence of the
Realm", shall be glad if you will
give this your attention? obliged

Mr Bailey
Done 27. 7. 16
HDa
27.

D

Yours faithfully,
[signature]
Station Supt.

Plate 117: This SECR letter of July 25 1916, refers to the enemy threat of Zeppelin raids. It is deciphered as follows: 'The City of London Electric Lighting Coy Ltd, 1 Great Winchester St, London EC, Reversal of the Globes of your Electric Lights, which during the night require blackening, to meet the requirements of the "Defence of the Realm", shall be glad if you will give this your attention.' (Note the rubber stamps and notes.)

Plate 118: Near **Oakley**, one of a series of large hoardings in fields by the West of England main line through Wessex. To the uninitiated, it is not obviously an advertisement for beer. Cheers!

Plate 119: Near **Binegar**, A cast-iron Somerset & Dorset sign in the heavy style of the LSWR, but with square corners instead of the rounded ones seen in *plate 120*. Do take care!

Plate 120: An example of an LSWR cast iron sign whose 'L', '&' and 'W' have been painted over. At **West Moors**, the single-line token is being collected by the driver of a standard class 4 Mogul No. 76054, to take his train up the Fordingbridge line to Salisbury. The signal box window panes contrast with the far end (see *plate 180*).

Plate 121: Two types of enamelled sign at **Bramley & Wonersh**: the station name between SR concrete posts and a books-by-post advertisement on the wooden wall of W.H. Smith. This contractor's line was taken over by the LBSCR, but the platform canopy and glazed end-partition are in pure LSWR tradition (see *plate 58*).

Plate 122: A badly chipped, BR enamelled sign at **Brasted**. The posters are mutually defeating, one promoting rail travel, the other promoting car travel. Alas, the inglorious M25 motorway now roars nearby this location.

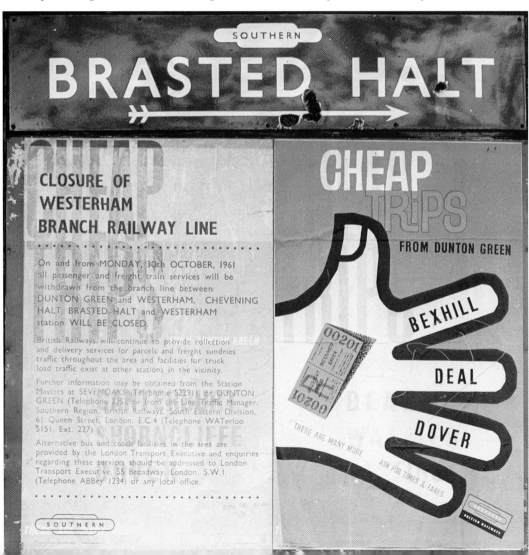

Plate 123: **Brasted** was one of the few Southern stations to display its name in whitened stones. This was all the more commendable since it had become an unmanned halt. The grassy bank and hedgerow are a delight, so too the canopy whose valance is non-standard for the SER, no doubt chosen by the contractor.

Plate 124: A pre-cast concrete name sign with three support posts, of the type introduced by the SR in the mid-1920s and manufactured at Exmouth Junction Works. A push-pull train at **Hurst Green Halt**, propelled by class H tank No. 31544, is about to take the direct line via Hever to Tunbridge Wells West (See also *plate 57*)

Plate 125: Seasonal good will and great value for money. The rounded corners were the easiest to pocket.

(S.T. 4.) Stock.

Application Form.

SOUTHERN RAILWAY.

No. 7321 ....Station.

....192...

Please supply me with a*.....................Rate

Season Ticket in favour of..............................

Address ....

....

Dated from ....192..... to

.......................192..... between your

Station and ....

advising me the charge to collect for it.

..............................Station Master.

To ....Station.

* Here insert "Full" or "Half."

NOTE.—This Application Form to be retained and carefully
preserved by the Station supplying the ticket.

(S.T. 4.) Stock

Dr. Transfer Voucher.

SOUTHERN RAILWAY.

No. 7321 ....Statio

....192.

DEAR SIR,

SEASON TICKET NO..............................

I enclose the above Ticket and am accounting for same on my Season Tick
Return for the month of.........................192.... Please bri
the value of the Ticket, viz., £ ....to Debit on your Season Ticket Accou
Current for the same month, and should the ticket not be taken up until the follow
month, include the amount in the Balance to next month as "Value of Tick
Outstanding."

Please complete the form appended hereto and return same to me immediately

Yours truly,

Mr..

....Station.

NOTE.—This Voucher to be sent to the Audit Accountant attached to Form S.T. 9 w
the Monthly Season Ticket Account Current.

(S.T. 4.) Stock

Cr. Transfer Voucher.

SOUTHERN RAILWAY.

No. 7321 ....Statio

....192.

DEAR SIR,

SEASON TICKET NO..............................

I acknowledge receipt of above and will bring value of sam
viz., £ ....to Debit on my Season Ticket Accou
Current for ....192......

Yours truly,

Mr. ....

....Station.

NOTE.—This Voucher to be sent to the Audit Accountant attached to Form S.T. 9 w
the Monthly Season Ticket Account Current

7 Signal Miscellany

Together with the frontispiece (*plate 1*), this chapter begins with a fine collection of LCDR signalry – always looking stately with their distinctive 'Ace of Spades' finials. The LCDR lines to Sheerness-on-Sea, Thanet and Dover were the first to lose their steam trains and semaphore signals after the Second World War. They were accordingly well photographed by the author during the transition period with both the old and the new in place. Because the LCDR (and SECR) used steel posts and iron finials (which were durable), many could still be found until 1959, although the arms were predominantly SR. By contrast, most SER wooden posts had rotted away long ago. Much rural LBSCR wooden signalry survived into the 1960s and these are featured in the author's first volume of *Odd Corners* (*Ref. 13*). A few LBSCR posts can also be spotted in other chapters of this volume (see *plates 65* and *194*).

From the late nineteenth century, the LSWR used durable metal posts and finials, so many of these also survived into the 1960s. Post-grouping, the LSWR designs were adopted for the SR as a whole, presenting challenges and puzzles for historians, regarding the precise origins of signals in the south-west. One way around this is to describe such assemblies as being *of LSWR design but with SR arms*.

Two designs of BR colour-light brackets are included, both greatly cantilevered. There is one GWR bracket, one S&D post, several SR girder brackets and many examples of SR rail-built posts. Interesting signalry can also be found throughout the other chapters. Their vivid colours and intriguing geometries were an integral part of the steam age.

Plate 126: As part of the 1959 Modernisation Programme, the platforms at **Faversham** were extended and realigned to take 12-car EMUs. One short-term problem was that the water crane could no longer reach the Up loop (left). In a section of new platform, LCDR lattice signal posts (tall and short) were fenced off, shortly to be dismantled. The great pointed finials were an endearing feature of the LCDR. One cluster of BR colour-lights is ready to take over, mounted precariously at the end of an extremely long lattice cantilever. The early SR electric lamps and name signs have apparently escaped modernisation, so too their LCDR fluted standards. The new pre-cast Down island platform (right) stands out against the LCDR brick out-buildings in the yard beyond.

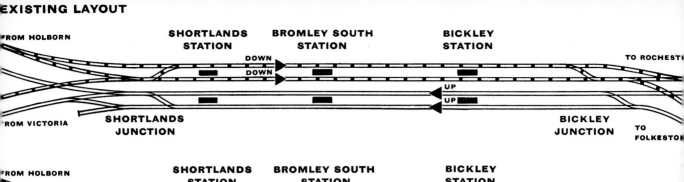

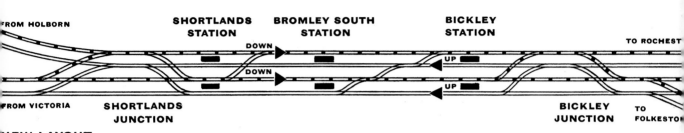

NEW LAYOUT

DOWN LINE ═══════

UP LINE ═══════

THESE two diagrams show the last engineering job to be done before the new services start two weeks from today.

The work was due to end at four o'clock this morning, for the rearranged lines between Shortlands and Swanley to come into use.

Until this week-end the lines ran in pairs—up, up, down, down (top diagram)—which meant that some up trains crossed the paths of some down trains.

With the new arrangement—up, down, up, down (bottom diagram) —and the quadrupled lines between Bickley Junction and Swanley, trains can cross at more than one point, which cuts out the bottlenecks at the junctions.

The switchover also means that from today many trains calling at Shortlands, Bromley South, Bickley and St. Mary Cray will leave from different platforms. The changes are shown on train departure sheets.

Biggest part of the job was rebuilding the junctions in the Bickley-Petts Wood area, where four main lines meet and diverge.

Three of the loop lines had to be moved because they curved too sharply and carried speed limits. Seven new bridges and culverts were built and 125,000 tons of earth were shifted. Forty-nine sets of points and 123 crossings were laid.

The work was done mainly during Saturday nights, when the junctions were closed to trains and special buses were run instead.

This week-end the junctions were closed from Saturday morning —for the last time. There were widespread train cancellations and diversions.

For the next few days trains will have to run slowly over these new lines. That means more delays. Remember, we don't run trains slowly for fun—it's for safety.

Plate 129 (*above*): **Shortland**'s Up fast home signals are SR corrugated, mounted on a balanced LCDR lattice bracket, shortly before the change to colour-lights. Work is in progress by the barrow crossing on what looks like a new concrete lamp standard. Workmen's equipment includes barrows, old sleepers, drain pipes and a sawhorse.

Plate 127 (*opposite, above*): Track diagrams from *South-East Report No. 5*, showing the change from UUDD to UDUD in the **Bromley** area, part of the Phase 1 Modernisation Programme to the Kent Coast. This newspaper was issued two weeks before the last steam train was due to depart Victoria at 8.52 pm on 14 June 1959. A personal message from Line Traffic Manager, Mr P.A. White, apologises for train delays over the previous few years and looks forward to a railway of which 'all can be proud'. But he warns 'Don't expect miracles overnight with the new streamlined services'. The author recalls that there were regular commuting delays on these services a decade later!

Plate 128 (*opposite, below*): A contrast of signalry at the country end of **Bromley South**. Three starting semaphores are carried on an SR balanced lattice bracket, while a new BR left-hand bracket carries colour-lights for the new Down fast line, almost obscuring the Up banner repeaters. New electric lamps and standards have been installed in 'art deco' style (inherited from the SR). A feature not apparent in *plate 127* is that the three trailing crossovers are of SR vintage. Note the concrete retaining wall, trunk telegraph poles and winter trees.

Plate 130 (*left*): An LCDR lattice post just outside **Ashford West**, carrying an SR 'advanced starter'. The subsidiary arm (a red ring over a short white arm) is for entry to an industrial siding and looks like an LCDR original.

Plate 132 (*above*): New colour-lights and a telephone box at **Brixton**. Discarded arms behind the LCDR lamp standard once adorned the LCDR lattice post on the right. It was a mountaineering feat to erect posts on such a viaduct.

Plate 131 (*opposite, below*): An odd corner of **Herne Hill Sorting Sidings**. The great SR cantilevered signal bracket is of girder construction, strengthened at the corner and steadied by two guys from above. The semaphore is wire-operated via pulleys. Other railway features are the water tower, a fenced dock, two simple water columns and an SR concrete loading gauge. A telegraph cable crosses the tracks. Note the mansard roof of the house beyond.

Plate 133 (*below*): At the country end of **Grove Park**, three very short SR semaphore starters served the Down fast line, guarding points to the Down slow line and the Bromley North branch. A Hastings DMU service crosses the latter (right). Workmen's equipment includes a cement mixer and ladders for the erection of a new colour-light gantry. The enamelled signs and concrete posts are SR, as are the rail-built signal posts with 'flat-cap' finials.

Plate 134: At the London end of **Denmark Hill**, a change of signalry on the Catford Loop. A cluster of four-aspect colour-lights is about to be erected on a new tubular steel post, replacing the delightful SR semaphore arms which are unusually short. The concrete hut may once have been for fogmen, but its door and warning suggest storage. Note the sheer brick cutting wall and the proximity of the suburban mansions alongside.

Plate 135 (*opposite*): **Mitcham Junction** was re-signalled in 1928 with a new SR signal box and lattice posts. This right-hand bracket carries the Down starters. The red-and-white subsidiary has an 'S' for 'entry into sidings' and carries the maker's inscription: *No. 1, S Ry, Henry Williams Ltd, Darlington*. The straight single line ahead is for West Croydon, while the main line to Sutton veers off sharply to the right at 20 mph. The Surrey Iron Railway once ran through here, horse-drawn upon stone sleepers, opening in 1803 and closing in 1846. It was the world's first *public* railway, although for goods only. The Wimbledon and Croydon Railway followed part of the old course, opening in 1855 and shortly absorbed into the LBSCR (see *plate 17* and *Ref. 5*).

Plate 137 (*above*): The LSWR installed pneumatic signals at **Salisbury** in 1902. The East box was upgraded by the SR with new electro-pneumatic semaphores (*Ref. 7*). This starter on a lattice post serves the Bournemouth bay. The air cylinder is seen below the balance arm. The Market House goods branch dives down to the right past the East box – a brick-built LSWR Type 4, but with a flat concrete roof added as an air-raid precaution during the Second World War.

Plate 136 (*left*): A lower-quadrant S&D 'distant' signal at **Masbury**, with its distinctive pointed finial carried on a post of two old rails bolted together (without the gap found on SR posts). Overhead wires supply the lamp.

Plate 138: At the country end of **East Dulwich**, this classic SR signal assembly comprises two flat, steel semaphore arms mounted on a post of two old bullhead rails – tied at intervals and topped with a cast iron cap, almost flat. The balance weight is suspended from an unusually short arm. The fogman's hut faces the wrong way for signal observation. Lighting and telegraph cables are from the signal box on the right (see *plate 164*).

Plate 139: A tall lattice signal post with a spiked, open finial of LSWR design, located on the Hayling branch. It is dual-purpose, carrying two ladders for the SR corrugated arms – 'fixed distant' for Havant and Home for **Langston**, whose platform can be seen in the distance. The lamps appear to be oil-lit.

Plate 140: Changes in BR ownership may well be reflected in the signalry at **Cattewater Junction**, alongside the River Plym on the outskirts of Plymouth. A tubular steel bracket of GWR design comes off the LSWR Cattewater goods branch (left), while an LSWR lattice bracket comes off the Laira Bridge from the Turnchapel and Yealmpton branches (right). The LSWR post is the taller and carries several steadying guys. Cattewater was actually two junctions with the signal box in between (*plate 179*). The missing semaphore arms are for the closed GWR spur to Mount Gould, leading to the GWR main line to North Road. The two remaining arms are for the LSWR spur to Plymouth Friary. Only freight traffic remained here when this picture was taken in 1959.

Plate 141: Two types of signal post were common on the LSWR. The earlier type comprised a square wooden post with a solid, wooden, circular, pointed finial. Other Victorian railways also used this type, McKenzie & Holland was a frequent supplier. The later and more durable type comprised a lattice, steel post with an open, four-sided, iron spike of a finial – a familiar combination, which became standard for the SR as a whole. This Home signal bracket at **Bodmin North** is an unusual hybrid of both types, probably dating from the station's re-opening in 1895. The semaphore arms are lower quadrant, wooden, slightly tapered and long. The main post carries the 'stop' signal, while the subsidiary on the platform has an open ring with white dot for 'entry into sidings'. The road bridge is similar to those seen at Brasted and Ashford (*plates 188* and *191*) but using stone masonry and with side plates instead of railings. Note the high crossing of the road and railway telegraphs.

Plate 142: At **Wadebridge**, a balanced bracket of LSWR lattice design, carrying four SR starting semaphores. The raised arm is for the local train to Bodmin North – a shiny set of Maunsells headed by Adams 0–4–4 class O2 tank No. 30236. Competing for attention is Beattie 2–4–0 well-tank No. 30587, on yard duty (see *plate 94*).

Plate 143: **Crowhurst** was remodelled by the SR with two bays, two platform loops and two through lines. Alas, traffic did not grow as expected and this grand junction for Bexhill West became a 'white elephant' in the middle of nowhere. The Down starting gantry is of light girder construction, reinforced by tie rods and steadied from either side by guys from subsidiary posts. It is impressive for both the proliferation of arms and the extensive use of white paint. The SER signal box stands like a rock in an ocean of trackwork, signals and platforms.

Plate 144: At **Yeovil Junction**, a massive balanced bracket of LSWR design with six SR starting semaphores for the Up through, Up local and Up loop, as well as one banner repeater for the Down through. The great cantilevered platform has two sets of steadying tie rods from a tall central post. The latticework is comparable with the finest lace. A Yeovil Town push-pull train of LSWR 'Ironclad' stock is propelled by a class M7 tank.

Plate 145: Signal posts and brackets look their best when painted white, even though the end may be blackened with locomotive soot. At **Fareham**, this left-hand bracket is of LSWR design, carrying three SR starting signals for the lines to Southampton (left), Eastleigh (avoiding the tunnel) and Eastleigh (via Tapnage tunnel). To fit the space available, the corrugated arms are shorter than standard. Other items of interest are the mobile yard crane (left), a Sugg Rochester gas lamp (centre) and the gantry crane (right) for containers of the original type.

Plate 146: At **Tonbridge**, this stately SR lattice bracket carries the Home signals from the Redhill line. Left to right, the dolls are for the bay, the Down loop, the Down through and a 'distant' arm for the Hastings line. Their method of operation appears to be mixed, with four motor boxes and two wire-pulleys visible. They date from the 1935 remodelling of the junction, as does the great brick signal box beyond with its elevated closet.

8   Signal Boxes and Crossings

While no reference book can cover every signal box variation since the year 'dot', *Reference 6* by the Signalling Study Group comes closest to it. Editor Peter Kay and other contributors not only define the principles of signal boxes and their contents, but also provide a wealth of illustrations of the common types built by railway companies and specialist contractors, with dates of production and general locations, nationwide. This chapter uses the type classifications defined by the SSG.

Some signal boxes do not fall readily into neat classification, being one-offs or hybrids of several types. Thanks are due to George Prior, railway historian and author, for helping to unravel the Botley window pane puzzle. One wonders what was the thinking in developments and designs. Were there internal battles between traditionalists and innovators? Were materials dictated by company financial constraints? Were there attempts to make each box 'special'? Alas, such records do not exist. What is clear is that aesthetics were an important consideration, the signal box being a proud ambassador of a company image.

Plate 147: Shepherds Lane had an SR Type 14 signal box built during the 1940s. ARP features (Air Raid Precautions) include brick construction, a flat, concrete roof and steel frames for the corner windows. The only ornamentation is the rendered waistband, carrying the name-plate. Is that a fifth-columnist with the camera? Call out the Home Guard – Captain Mainwaring will soon put a stop to it! The box closed in 1959. Chalk graffiti announce the last day for sale to be '7 March, apply LED office, Queer Street, best offer over 10/-'.

Plate 148: An unusual brick signal box at **Ashford West** viewed from the rear. The main windows, locking room window heads and horizontal boarding under the gable indicate McKenzie & Holland design. The box is dilapidated, with peeling paint, encroaching ivy and windows either blacked out, broken or filthy. Nevertheless, it retains a proud air by virtue of solid form, fine brickwork and a tall, ornate brick chimney. (Stovepipes superseded chimneys from the late nineteenth century.) The catwalk almost encircles the box. Note the wheelbarrows and platelayers' trolleys stacked against the rear wall, part of the 'way out west' frontier image.

Plate 149: **Sheerness-on-Sea** had a small Saxby & Farmer Type 5 box with horizontal boarding, a hipped roof, a catwalk without toe-board, tall window panes in blocks of four and a row of narrow top-lights. The rounded corners of the windows are a distinct S&F characteristic. The platform is for the token exchange. Foreground debris is for electrification and the change to colour-lights. The box, recently closed, is being demolished.

Plate 150 (*below*): The new BR power box at **Shepherds Lane** (Brixton) was one of eight which replaced thirty-one mechanical boxes on the LCDR main line in 1959. Brick-built with a flat roof, its large, sliding single-pane windows are cleaned by leaning out. Stairs are internal, so is the washroom behind the name sign. Overall, it is an assemblage of Lego blocks with projecting roofs, leaving an impression of bland modernity. It was photographed shortly after opening in 1959. See *plate 108* for the view east from the operating room.

Plate 151 (*left*): **Adisham** had a tall, narrow, wooden signal box of LCDR in-house design, with vertical boarding, a gabled roof, a catwalk with toe-boards, and many small window panes in blocks of twelve – spotlessly clean, unlike the locking room window below. Like Harrietsham, the lever frame faces the running lines. Later frames usually faced away from running lines, since the block boards (suspended above the frame) became too full, causing line obscuration.

Plate 152 (*right*): **Haywards Heath** had an early SR brick signal box with horizontal boarding below the gabled roof. The asymmetric window panes may be compared with those at Mitcham Junction of the same era (*plate 135*). There is a closet on the balcony. The locking room windows are bricked up and a concrete cable-channel rises over the point rodding. The platform canopy is of plain SR design, sloping inwards to a central gutter. The ancient cast-iron lamp standard is LBSCR – straight-fluted with floral ornamentation. Originally carrying an oil lamp, it has been converted to gas with a swan-neck pipe, a top tap (operated by pole) and a Sugg Rochester lamp. The standard also carries a name sign, a loudspeaker and a speaker insulator. To its right is the roof of the subway stairs.

Plate 153: **Harrietsham**'s McKenzie & Holland signal box has a brick locking room, horizontal boarding to a gabled roof with little overhang, no catwalk and window panes in blocks of four and six. Two pointed finials appear to have been cropped. Unlike Sheerness, there is no porch. The white-painted LCDR lattice post carries an SR starting signal. The Ashford West line escaped signal modernisation when it was electrified in 1961.

Plate 154: This stately overhead signal box at **Orpington** spans a siding like a carriage-washing shed. The lower brick walls are elegant with oval apertures. The box itself is of standard SER design with horizontal boards, a hipped roof and a locking room with brick end-walls. All are mounted upon cross-beams of concrete and steel. It is a long climb to the unporched door. It must have been an unenviable job to clean the windows from the narrow catwalk at the front. The locking room windows were presumably never cleaned.

Plate 156 (*opposite, below*): The squat, overhead signal box at **Holborn Viaduct** was built on steel girders across the 1 in 39 incline to Moorgate and Farringdon. The box is of LCDR design with a new mechanism installed by the SR in 1926. It has horizontal boarding, a hipped roof, a catwalk with toe-boards and many sliding windows of four panes. Colour-light signals, also of 1926 vintage, were the first four-aspect installation in the world. They are mounted on a tubular steel post with a 'dunces hat' finial. The buildings beyond bristle with vent pipes and chimneys, topped by the 'wedding cake' spire of Sir Christopher Wren's St Bride's church, just off Fleet Street.

Plate 155: The joint LSWR/LBSCR junction station at **Epsom** was remodelled by the SR with two wide island platforms. The great overhead signal box is supported between the platforms on girders of enormous span. This looks an expensive solution, compared with building a tall box from the centre of one of the platforms. The box itself is of early SR design, incorporating features inherited from the LSWR – horizontal boarding, a hipped roof and a delightful configuration of window panes and top lights. In place of a catwalk, there are safety-rails to lean on while sitting on the sills to clean the windows. The 4-SUB train is bound for London Bridge.

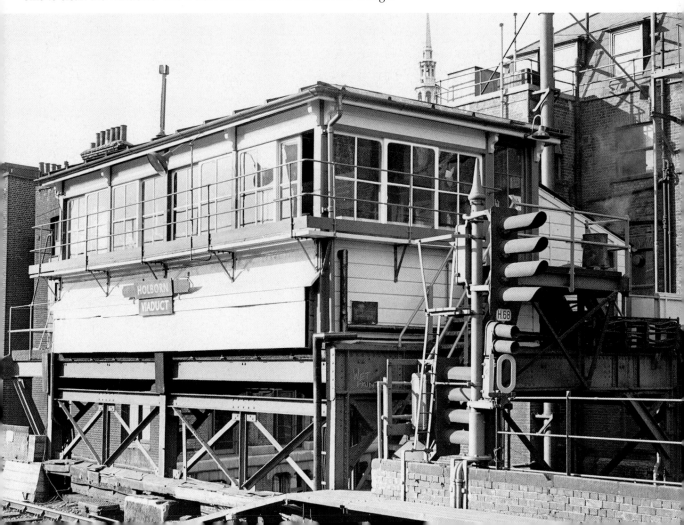

Plate 157: This SR level-crossing near **Gomshall** has concrete posts, oil lamps, X-bracing and metal netting. It is controlled by an unusual SER signal box – a tall crow's nest with horizontal barge-boards, SER windows and a flat roof. A simple canopy has been added to make a rudimentary porch. Note the multi-spar trunk telegraph.

Plate 158: The **Headcorn** box is of early SR design – brick-built with a gabled roof and asymmetric window panes, a geometry similar to Haywards Heath. No closet is apparent, but there is an entrance porch at the front – an odd arrangement, partially obscuring the line. Viewed from a rear quarter, the locking room windows are clear, also the extension (under construction) for new power signalling equipment. A cement mixer is mounted on the flat wagon, with scaffolding and planks for barrowing. The SR Up starting signals can be seen in the distance.

Plate 159: **Cliffe** had a classic vernacular signal box of SER in-house design with horizontal barge-boards, a hipped roof and large, vertically-sliding windows of single panes. There is no catwalk – windows were cleaned either by using a short ladder or by sitting on the sill from the inside. (Preserved at the NRM, York, the operating room of Borough Market junction box has cradle bars above each sill for safe cleaning.) The matching shelter is of a simple design with a sloping roof, cantilevered over the platform and carrying an SER suspended oil lamp. Wooden rectangularity is relieved by the quaint metal stovepipe and two oil-drum flower tubs.

Plate 160: The IWR used a mix of S&F, Stevens and in-house signal box designs. The Bembridge branch was pure Stevens. The junction box at **Brading**, however, was of IWR in-house design, but with Stevens windows (see also *plate 3*). Tall and brick-built, the hipped roof has an endearing valance on three sides. The windows have horizontal panes, three deep, believed to be originals. Closed in 1953, a siding once ran across the foreground by the timber bridge (left) where only a few rods and wires remain. Note the flowers in the windows of the operating room.

Plate 161: **St Johns** signal box is early SR – brick-built with a gabled roof and curly, wooden eaves brackets. The upper lights are panelled and ten window panes have been covered up to reduce sun glare. The narrow catwalk looks precarious. The locking room has extensions for power equipment and has lost its windows. Three men in shirt-sleeves are at work. Viewed from the embankment of Parks Bridge, a forest of Victorian chimney pots can be seen beyond, also a bridge (above the box) of the closed LCDR branch to Greenwich Park.

Plate 162: At **Merstone**, access to the island platform was from the middle of the level-crossing. Passengers were protected by railings and were no doubt escorted by a railwayman (see also *plate 87*). Four years after closure, the SR gates and the water tower still look serviceable, but the fine old signal box had been vandalised. The box is brick-built with boarding at the gable ends. Although lacking finials, the bargeboards, main windows and gable window indicate the builder to be the Railway Signalling Company, the usual contractor for the IWCR. See *plate 105* for the RSCo box at Newport.

Plate 163: A peaceful platform scene at **Cranleigh**, with the signal box, an open gate and a lady's bicycle. There is a church steeple in the distance beyond the coal yard and barns. The box is Saxby & Farmer Type 3b, built in 1875 of vertical battened boarding upon a brick base and with a stove-pipe chimney. The small porch looks like an add-on. The paintwork is in pristine condition and the windows are gleaming (see also *plate 65*).

Plate 164: Saxby & Farmer signal boxes predominated on the LBSCR. From 1880, however, some in-house designs were built. LBSCR Type 3b was introduced in 1899, having large sliding windows, two panes deep. Other characteristics strongly resemble Evans, O'Donnell designs of that era, including the finials, horizontal boarding, a louvre vent in the gable end, the roof overhang, the catwalk, its supporting brackets and the locking room window design. **East Dulwich** is an example of this type – the setting looks so rural! (See also *plate 50*.)

Plate 165: **Crystal Palace** low-level station was rebuilt in 1875. Seen on the approach from Sydenham, the 'C' box looks like a late example of a Saxby & Farmer Type 1b. The narrow band of small window panes and the low-pitched hipped roof are also reminiscent of early LSWR boxes (*plate 58*). To its right are the trunk telegraph, a platelayers' hut and allotment gardens with a grounded LBSCR coach body. EMU storage sidings are to the left and right.

Plate 166: **Rudgwick** signal box is a variation of LBSCR Type 3b. It resembles East Dulwich (*opposite*) in most respects except three: the wavy bargeboard at the gable end, the windows of three panes across instead of the more usual two, and the lapped boarding which extends to the ground level instead of stopping at the locking room windows. The brackets supporting the landing and catwalk are clear in this picture. Approaching from the Horsham direction is Wainwright 0–4–4 class H tank No. 31322 with an SECR ten-compartment third.

Plate 167: At **Peckham Rye**, tucked away at the eastern end of the Catford Loop Down platform, is the tiny 'B' signal box which closed in 1959. Since there were no sidings or junctions on these LCDR lines, the prime function of the box was to operate signals. The position of the old nameplate is clear and the woodwork looks as though it was never repainted from new. Cable channels rise above former signal wires. (See also *plate 41.*)

Plate 168: It is not obvious why the 'C' box at **Peckham Rye Junction** was rebuilt in 1899 (a good five years before work might have started on track rearrangements for the new electric train sheds). The vast majority of LBSCR boxes were built by Saxby & Farmer, but others appeared between 1898 and 1901. This looks like an LBSCR hybrid. The arrow-head finials, gabled roof and rectangular end-vent are Evans, O'Donnell features, but the windows are S&F Type 10. The top half has horizontal boards (in need of painting). The locking room is solid brick with no front windows, but it blends quite well with suburbia beyond.

Plate 169: Peckham Rye 'A' box was built in 1880, replacing an earlier box on the opposite side of the tracks. It is an LBSCR Type 2a, having an overhung hipped roof and 'baroque' features of full valancing and a large central vent. The chimney alongside looks modern, possibly from commercial premises below. Cow Lane coal sidings (right) were opened in 1891, jointly owned by the MR and LNWR, with a wagon hoist to ground level. The SR signal bracket is grimy but delightful, carrying one 'stop', one 'distant' and one short red-and-white subsidiary arm for 'entry into sidings'. Note the safety chains on the balance weights. Three LBSCR platforms were originally controlled from here – two Up and one Down. The South London Line's centre track (for empty stock working) was lifted in 1933. Cow Lane sidings became disused in 1958 and the 'A' box closed in 1965.

Plate 170: Wybourne Siding signal box was named after the associated farm. It controlled the private siding as well as farm crossing gates and the associated stop signals of **High Halstow** halt. As at Beluncle (*opposite, below*), the SECR halt was added in 1906, post-dating the box. Classic SER design features include the black-on-white name sign, lapped barge-boards, a hipped roof and vertical sliding windows of two panes. Note the wire-tensioning arm in the foreground, the quaint stove-pipe chimney and the gate to the rich, ploughed field beyond.

Plate 171 (*opposite, above*): Not a pixie's house but an LSWR signal box covering the ground-frame at **Daggons Road**. Fairy features include the curved pointed roof, multiple small window panes, cut-out wooden lettering and the sylvan setting. The horizontal boarding is characteristic of LSWR Type 1, the windows are Type 2 and the roof is unique. It controlled movements into and out of the sidings. A shunting pole is leaning on the railing.

Plate 172 (*opposite, below*): **Miskin Siding** signal box was named after one of the line's supporters (*Ref 8*) and housed a small ground frame. It is a Stevens design, having a brick base, vertical boarding below a gabled roof and horizontal window panes. Stevens was an occasional signal box supplier to the SER until about 1884 (*Ref 6*). The Hundred of Hoo Railway opened in 1882, so Miskin is a late (and rare) example of Stevens on the SER. The enamelled name sign is SER, similar to Wybourne (*opposite*). The loading gauge is SER, but **Beluncle Halt** alongside was an after-thought, opened by the SECR in 1906.

Plate 173: **Holme Crossing**, near Wool, has a late-LSWR signal box with a ground-frame, identified by its round-topped window panes as Type 4. A vent and a stove-pipe chimney rise from the hipped roof, in contrast with the brick chimney of the crossing-keeper's house beyond. The tall, white-painted lattice signal posts are of LSWR design, but the steel semaphore arms and concrete hut are SR. The level-crossing gates are difficult to characterise, having an unusual central diamond and single diagonal bracing. (The common LSWR gate design had six bars with single diagonals and a central red disc.) This was a busy main line, built for high-speed running to Weymouth. Both tracks have concrete sleepers, but only one has flat-bottom rails (but not of long-welded).

Plate 175 (*opposite, below*): The earliest signal boxes were little more than refuges, built alongside an open-air ground-frame. This refuge hut at **Langston** resembles a Saxby & Farmer Type 1b box, having a hipped roof, horizontal lapped boarding and sliding windows, two panes deep, in sympathy with the house opposite. It guards a busy road crossing whose SR gates are exceptionally long because of the skew. Cast-iron SR notices beyond warn against Trains and Trespass. Note the tall SR yard lamp, the modest telegraph and the vegetable patch. The platform entrance gate is on the right. Opened in 1867, the Hayling Railways Company was originally independent, with both the LBSCR and LSWR having running powers. It was taken over by the LBSCR in 1872, but the six-lever ground frame (just to the right of the hut) remained clearly cast 'LSWR'.

Plate 174: Overshadowed by a great ash tree, this modest, but picturesque crossing-keeper's cottage near **Betchworth** guards the southern approach to Kemp's Farm. It has three tall chimneys, TV/radio aerials, gabled roof overhangs, rounded window heads, a telephone box and a birdcage in the open porch. An Up train of BR and Bulleid stock is headed by class N Mogul No. 31852. Amid the spring flowers, the SECR warns against trespass, while the SR advises to 'Stop, Look and Listen'. For such a modest farm-crossing, the provisions and operating costs seem excessive by modern standards; the keeper's lifestyle must have been idyllic.

Plate 178 (*above*): **Downton** had a classic LSWR Type 1 box, built of horizontal boarding upon a brick base and with an ornate brick chimney. The hipped roof has a pair of globular finials (one broken) and once carried an ornate valance. There is no catwalk. Modifications include a new wooden staircase, the covered balcony and entrance porch with a closet projecting at the rear. Rods and wires emerge from beneath the platform end-ramp. The box was relegated in 1922 for goods movements only and looks as though it was never repainted again.

Plate 176 (*opposite, above*): The operating room at **Raynes Park** is an LSWR Type 2, having a hipped roof, top-lights and sliding windows of six panes. The eaves would once have had a valance. As an Air Raid Precaution during the 1940s, an anti-blast plain brick wall was built around the locking room. The great catwalk acts as a sort of membrane between the two incongruous halves. A wooden staircase brings visual relief, so too the porch with its integral WC and water-tank – clad, boarded and supported on timber stilts. Note the clusters of cables and rows of houses beyond.

Plate 177 (*opposite, below*): The imposing **Plymouth Friary** 'A' box is an LSWR Type 3b, brick-built with a hipped roof, a catwalk and 168 window panes: 120 on the front and twenty-four on each side. The large locking room window has been bricked up. A substantial platform is for the token exchange, complete with an SR yard lamp. Note the central vent in the roof and an H type stove-pipe at the rear.

Plate 181 (*above*): Apart from the windows, **Botley** signal box is a standard LSWR Type 1, featuring a hipped roof, six horizontal lapped boards upon a brick base and vertical boards for the porch. This example also has a catwalk with substantial railings. The horizontal window panes, three deep, are BR replacements, probably installed in 1958 when a new lever frame was fitted. The originals would have been small panes, two deep (see *plate 178*). The wooden veranda has classic X bracing for the rail and carries a coal bin, fire buckets and the entry porch.

Plate 179 (*opposite, top*): **Cattewater Junction** had a late LSWR Type 4 box – timber but without a central pillar. It has a hipped roof, no catwalk, but a balcony for the token exchange (worthy of Shakespeare's Juliet). Clear LSWR characteristics are the name sign and main windows of four panes, the upper ones being round-headed. The wooden cut-out letters are crystal clear, painted white upon a black board. (See also *plate 141*.)

Plate 180 (*opposite, below*): **West Moors** had an LSWR Type 3b box – having deeper windows than Type 1 and horizontal boarding instead of top-lights. The near-end (horizontal) window panes look like Stevens but are probably BR replacements (see *plate 120*). The box is of plain brick with a hipped roof, an ornamental vent and no catwalk. Other railway features are Railway Dwelling No. 19 (nicely finished in white), crossing gates (without the usual X bracing), the huge trunk telegraph, a tall LSWR signal post and one of the earliest LSWR concrete footbridges – whose graceful, slender arch with iron railings contrasts with the angular, heavy design with concrete sides which became standard for the SR (see *plate 56*). The junction signal bracket can be seen in the distance.

Plate 182: **Shillingstone** box is an S&D version of LSWR Type 2, having deeper windows than Type 1, vertical boarding below the windows and horizontal boarding for the locking room. The restfulness of the hipped roof is echoed in the squat hut with its frilly valance, whose main purpose appeared to be for bicycle storage. Note the Whittaker automatic token collection devices on either side of the running lines.

Plate 183: The **Glastonbury and Street** box is a variation of a late-LSWR Type 4, having horizontal boarding with a central panel for the operating room. Customisation for the S&D includes a valanced porch and ornate vents on the hipped roof. The four-pane round-topped sliding windows are identical to those at Cattewater Junction (*plate 179*). It is sparkling clean – even the rods are visible through the locking room windows. Affixed to the front are an SR name sign, three fire buckets, a wooden box, a bicycle and a gas lamp. There is neat planking for the barrow crossing and over the rods and wires. There was once a water column by the platform railing.

Plate 184: This smart-looking box at **Blandford Forum** is an S&D variation of a late-LSWR Type 4, having a central front timber panel between round-topped windows of four panes. The medium-pitch gabled roof, with large overhang, creates a quite different overall appearance from the mellow hipped roofs which are more usual on the LSWR. The provision of a catwalk is a further variation. The catwalk and side-balcony are supported on elegant iron brackets. Fine finishing touches are the multipane locking room windows, the valanced entrance porch and the bracing of the wooden staircase and balcony. Note the two styles of S&D saw-tooth valancing for the Up and Down platform canopies, also the two-storey warehouse of the coal and coke merchant.

Plate 185: When the SR installed a crossing loop at **Haven Street** in 1926, a new single-storey station building was built, incorporating the signal box at one end. It has a ground frame of sixteen levers of which six were spare in 1960. The block board has two (different) bells, two plungers and two position indicators for the 'distant' signals. Alongside the Tyer electric key token apparatus is a 'pouch and hoop' for single line working to Newport. Ageing of the signal box window panes creates distortions in the SR cast-iron 'Beware' sign. This box remains in service today.

Plate 186: The Evans, O'Donnell signal box at **Ryde St Johns Road** was a hand-me-down from Waterloo Junction on the SECR. EOD features include the small window in the gable end and the asymmetric window panes. Such extensive glazing and no false ceiling suggest chilly corners in winter. The locking frame, facing away from the running lines, has forty-two levers, with many locked off for single-line winter working to Smallbrook junction. The cast lever nameplates are of the standard SR type, having different colours for functions. The telegraph beam has a multitude of electrical repeaters, bells and plungers for communication to the adjacent boxes at Ryde Esplanade, Smallbrook and Brading. All is clean, neat and tidy, even to the notices on the far board.

9 Bridges and Tunnels

This chapter shows some attractive steel bridges carrying the railway over roads, railway lines and a river. The long, skewed ones are bowed with massive sides of either plate or open truss type. They contrast with the simple short span beam bridges which are of much lighter construction. Road bridges over the railway are in brick and steel – see also *plates 140* and *226* in other chapters. Footbridges are shown in steel and wood, while other chapters show them in concrete (*plates 56* and *180*). The tunnel portals are of brick and stone.

With the exception of footbridges, there are no general design patterns. Road bridges, water bridges, viaducts and tunnel portals were generally one-offs to meet the particular needs of each situation, usually seeking the lowest capital cost consistent with safety and projected axle loadings. A few had fine architectural form or ornamentation to inspire public confidence. For the most part, however, the sheer mass of the structure was sufficient to impress the travelling public.

Bridge and portal designs may be of limited interest to the railway historian, but to the railway modeller, such detail is invaluable in planning and building a layout. A fine truss across the centre of a baseboard can be quite stunning. The American genius, John Allen, was a master of modelling bridges (*Ref. 9*). Built in HO gauge, his Gorre & Daphetid Railroad occupied 630 sq. ft of basement floor space, floor-to-ceiling with 130 bridges and fourteen tunnels in stunning, mountainous terrain.

Plate 187: The massive steel bow truss at **Battledown** carries the Southampton Up line over the West of England main lines, seen here with the Atlantic Coast Express, headed by 'Merchant Navy' class Pacific No. 35014 *Nederland Line*. Acting like the spokes of a wheel, this open type of construction looks lighter than the bow plate type seen at London Bridge (*plate 190*). The four brick pillars are extended purely for appearance.

Plate 188: This steel road bridge near **Brasted** is of light construction, having tall railings in place of the top plating seen at Ashford (opposite, below). Otherwise, the design principles are the same – brick abutments, deep H-girders at the side and cross-beams to carry the track. The telegraph follows the lane, burrowing under the railway by cable.

Plate 189: The LSWR's extension from Nine Elms to Waterloo is carried on a brick viaduct whose arches are used for storage and operational purposes. It is crossed (above and below) by other railways, including the LBSCR, LCDR, the West London and many service lines. This steel skew bridge connects the various yards at **Nine Elms** on either side of the main line. Items of interest are the LSWR shunting signal, the curved double-slip point and the water column and telegraph cables attached to the viaduct. The area was 100 per cent railway.

Plate 190: The SER's costly West End Extension to Charing Cross and Cannon Street required some massive bow bridges skewed over roads. This one crosses the **London Bridge** approach road, used here as an exit for buses and taxis. The great ribbed sides are of fabricated steel plate, supported on Portland stone abutments and on two rows of intermediate tubular steel columns. They carry cables along the top and are painted for both rust protection and advertising revenue. Note the oldstyle police cone (pyramid with chevrons) and the modern electric street lamp on the right. Most of the pedestrians are wearing flat caps, a fashion going back to the nineteenth century.

Plate 191: On the Hastings line at **Ashford**, a class H tank with a mineral wagon crosses a steel road bridge, dated 1901. Not even a single-deck bus could negotiate this low bridge. The road leads to the new town, built specifically for railway workers, and to the railway works whose entrance tower can be seen. Opened in 1850, Ashford superseded the SER works at New Cross and later the LCDR works at Longhedge, Battersea.

Plate 192: This LSWR girder footbridge at **Whitchurch North** has Warren trussing, wire netting along the sides and a Sugg Rochester gas lamp at either end. The Italianate building is substantial for such a country station of modest traffic. The deeply valanced LSWR rectangular canopy of the Down platform contrasts with the plain arc roof of the island canopy. Numerous LSWR barrows (mostly redundant) adorn the platforms.

Plate 193: Cox's Walk crosses the closed LCDR branch to Crystal Palace by an unusual footbridge just south of **Lordship Lane** station. Using two central brick plinths, three wooden trusses support the walkway, while smaller side-trusses support the lattice sides. Such designs were common in America. They are straightforward to model *in situ*, requiring balsa, glue, a knife and plenty of patience. This is a replacement bridge – the original was even more ornate, with ball finials and rustic sides. Alas, such bridges tend to rot and can also catch fire.

Plate 194: A panorama of **Lewes** from above the Brighton lines. The main building (left) and the great covered footbridge opened 1889. The platform lift is SR, so too the semaphore arms and the 'starting back' bracket on the left. The wooden 'balanced' bracket (right) is LBSCR. The station frontage is grand and welcoming, having a clerestoried booking hall, a large carriage canopy and a balustrade roofline with large ball finials. The twin platform faces of the loop line (left) are distinctly LBSCR. The station layout was designed to ease passenger transfers between services to London, Brighton, Seaford, Hastings, Tunbridge Wells and the Bluebell line. It is a huge station in a fine South Downs setting, with further platforms serving the lines to Haywards Heath.

Plate 195: The **Tavy** crossing from afar, carrying an air-smoothed Bulleid light Pacific on a short train to Plymouth. The central bow trusses have Warren girder sides, similar to Battledown, but the approach viaduct has brick arches, more akin to Nine Elms. This is one of the great flooded valleys of the south-west peninsula, with woodland on the convex hillsides reaching to the water's edge. The Tavy joined the Tamar here where sailing barges plied their trade in 1959.

Plate 196: This cast-iron notice by the LSWR main line in **Clapham Cutting** reads: 'The LOCOMOTIVE ACT 1861 – NOTICE IS HEREBY GIVEN that this bridge is insufficient to carry weights beyond the ORDINARY TRAFFIC of the District'. Such wording seems vague by modern standards. Judging by the bent railings, the main practical use of the sign was to assist trespassers and railway workers over the wall.

Plate 198: There were two tunnels on the LCDR branch to Crystal Palace, which opened in 1884 to serve the relocated Great Exhibition. The portal of Crescent Wood tunnel looks exceptionally tall at the London end of **Upper Sydenham** station. The fine brickwork and ornamentation could be appreciated from the platforms, although partly obscured by a covered footbridge. This led from the booking office above – a great Victorian red-brick mansion which also housed the stationman. The branch was electrified in 1925 and the palace burnt down in 1936; traffic declined and the branch closed in 1954. This sylvan, scrubby scene retains a country air.

Plate 197 (*opposite, below*): This brick road bridge at the London end of **Ashford** has four separate arches – a design cheaper to construct than one long span. Standard 2–6–4 class 4MT tank No. 80040 shunts assorted vans on the Down loop, looking much too large for the arch. Note the various grades of soot above the arches – only the Down 'through' line is clean. The signal dolls are SR, supported on what looks like a temporary gantry, pending the change to colour-lights. The water column beyond (between the Up lines) has lost its hose.

Plate 199 (*left*): The faced stone, low-roofed, single-track portal of **St Lawrence Tunnel** is part of the Ventnor West branch which closed in 1953. The tunnel curves to the right and was open for all to explore in 1960.

Plate 200 (*below*): Many tunnel portals were ornamented, but they remained unseen except for railway workers and the occasional enthusiast-photographer. Such was the southern end of **Somerhill Tunnel**, set among the silver birch of the High Weald between Tonbridge and High Brooms. A Hastings DMU emerges, having flat-sided Restriction 0 stock (8 ft) for the tunnels south of Tunbridge Wells. Somerhill tunnel is Restriction 1 (8 ft 6 in).

Plate 201: The south portal of **Sevenoaks Tunnel** is plainer and clearly wider than at Somerhill. Rebuilt 'West Country' class Pacific No. 34012 *Launceston* bursts forth with a train of Bulleid stock for the Channel ports. A tarpaulin has been draped over the wooden platelayers' hut and work is in progress for tunnel electrification and colour-light signalling. At night, this spot would be alive with construction workers. Wild spring flowers carpet the foreground. The telegraph is comprised of a multi-core cable that must have passed through the tunnel.

Plate 202: The station throat at the eastern end of **Tunbridge Wells West**. Guarded by the S&F signal box, all running lines converge for the first of a series of narrow tunnels through to the SER. At the end of the island platform are a water column, brazier and a pair of tall SR starting signals with low-level shunting discs. A mix of Bulleid and Maunsell coaches are stored on the right-hand siding. (Both pictures on this page feature a Bulleid brake-third.) The road bridge has weight restriction diamonds and the wooded hillside beyond has some tantalising glimpses of Victorian mansions. What a pleasure it must have been to amble down to the LBSCR for a ride on a steam train. This remains an attractive option today, courtesy of the Spa Valley Railway whose members operate vintage steam services as far as Groombridge.

10 Coaches, Sets and Units

The story of Southern coaches is one of evolution – from the inherited splendour of pre-group wood-panelled masterpieces – through the steel-clad era of the interwar years – to the all-steel designs of Mr Bulleid and BR. Each had charm and a purpose appropriate to the era in which it was built. This chapter presents a selection of bogie coaches built between about 1900 and 1960. Features and styles are compared and contrasted, including conversions to push-pull, electric, de-icing, open saloon, cafeteria, driver training and a farm shed. Hybrid coach combinations were also commonplace, found in push-pull sets, *ad hoc* corridor steam trains and in 'augmented' Electric Multiple Units (EMUs).

In order to show detail, most of the pictures are of single coaches. A few show more than one train. These have an additional appeal, especially appreciated by railway modellers – of the sight of one train slowly passing another. An extreme example of this is the massed storage sidings at Clapham Junction (below), with empty stock snaking miraculously from some hidden corner on to a running line. One can enjoy, too, the fine locomotives which accompany many of the coaches and sets.

Plate 203: A wealth of rolling stock in carriage sidings at **Clapham Junction**. Assorted vans are stored by the LSWR milk platform (top left). There is an early Bulleid corridor set (with side doors) in the shed. The nearest siding has a Maunsell set, including a restaurant car with curtains. The headboard beyond reads 'Newspaper Traffic Waterloo Ilfracombe'. LSWR 4–6–2 class H16 tank No. 30517 is on empty stock duty to Waterloo. The open baskets between the tracks appear to contain either coach litter or fresh accessories for restaurant cars.

Plate 204: Between 1905 and 1908, the LSWR built corridor coaches for emigrants to the USA, with overall dimensions to suit any port on any railway in Britain. This brake-third has been converted to push-pull with the addition of SR bogies, underframe and cab end. Beyond the lavatory window are four compartment doors, then double doors for luggage and a single cab/guard's door. It was not until the Bulleid regime of the early 1940s that side doors disappeared from main line compartments, thereby creating a modern image with panoramic windows.

Plate 205: The 'other half' of the push-pull set seen above – an LSWR 'emigrant' composite viewed from the corridor side. There are four doors, two blanks and a vestibule/lavatory at either end. These majestic main line coaches are relegated here to branch line duty with a Wainwright 0–4–4 tank. Note the long, plain wooden SR canopy of **Allhallows-on-Sea** terminus, dating from 1932. It looks as though it has never been repainted.

Plate 206: The LBSCR was one of a few companies to continue the low-arc roof into the era of bogie stock. When some were subsequently fitted with SR cab ends, they acquired a Stroudleyesque appearance, though they were actually from Robert Billinton's era. Set No. 716 is seen near **Redgate Mill Junction**, also spotted six months later on the Allhallows branch (*plate 55*). Fairburn 2–6–4 tank No. 42068 leads the way.

Plate 207: An SECR 50 ft 'birdcage' composite being restored in the bay at **Sheffield Park**. Painting is in progress along the gutter. Built at Ashford in 1909, this was originally part of a three-coach 'A' set for use on outer suburban services. There is no corridor or lavatory, but there were lavatories on the other two coaches. Note the hybrid panelling of rounded top panels (in SER style) and square-cornered waist panels (in LCDR style). Other items of interest are the lamp standard, oil lamp and water crane (all LBSCR) and the enamelled advertisement for oatmeal stout. The overall scene evokes the spirit of the early preservation movement.

Plate 208: A close-up of an LBSCR non-corridor composite. It has long, slender handrails and an almost flat side, whereas the SECR coach beyond has a wider waist and an elliptical roof. Also evident are the comforts and facilities of **Ventnor** terminus – a comprehensive canopy with ornate iron brackets – and discrete rooms for refreshments, ladies, waiting, parcels and cloaks. It is a welcoming place, well protected from the weather.

Plate 209: The interior of a third class saloon of an SECR coach on the Isle of Wight. There is seating for eighteen passengers, with the longitudinal benches each holding five. This coach was originally a 54 ft first/second composite, part of an 'A' set of 1910 vintage. The two central first-class compartments accommodated five passengers each and had interlacing lavatories. The lavatories and walls were removed at Lancing in 1948–49 to create these spacious saloons for Island service. They were used during the author's IOW school journey in 1951, with half the class packed, among much merriment and excitement, on an excursion to Freshwater.

Plate 210: This LSWR non-corridor brake-third from 1906 to 1910 has become a Departmental coach for breakdown duty, seen at **Exeter Central** with a class N Mogul. Note the long luggage compartment, the great ducket for the guard and a lavatory for one of the two central compartments. It is a pity that such coaches could not have been transferred to the Isle of Wight (instead of converting SECR stock with enlarged luggage compartments).

Plate 211: One half of a pre-group coach body which ended its days as a farm hut at **Godshill**. Precise identification is hampered by the metal cladding and the lack of an underframe, but the low-arc roof, square-cornered windows and hand-rail design indicate that it is LCDR, probably a bogie coach, since there would be little point in splitting a 4- or 6-wheeler. The Isle of Wight also had some PD&SWJR bogie coaches with the low-arc roof, but they had narrower door vents, less square window corners and different hand-rail fixings.

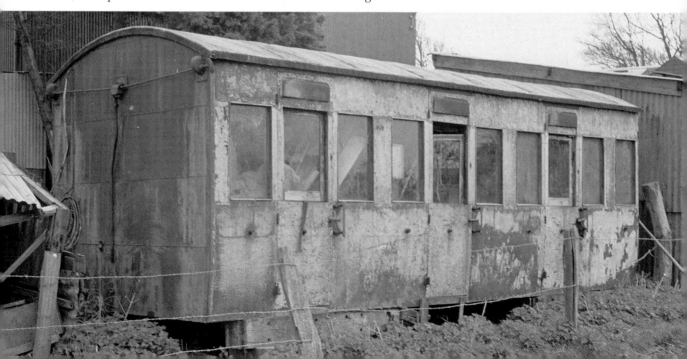

Plate 212: This romantic Edwardian scene at **Westerham** features the branch terminus, a Wainwright class H tank, push-pull set No. 482 and a stationman leaning on the fence – there was time to think in the days of steam. Each coach started life in 1906–7 as an SECR rail motor, being integral with a stubby 0–4–0 tank. They were converted into conventional push-pull sets in 1924 when steel panelling and inter-coach gangways were added. No. 482 served on branches to Bembridge, Gravesend West and Westerham (*Ref. 12*). They were scrapped in 1960, six months after this picture, and replaced by Maunsell push-pull sets.

Plate 213: The spacious interior of the far SECR coach seen in *plate 212*. This is a third class open saloon, with thirty-two low-back seats. Beyond the sliding door is the former first class saloon with ten seats. The author's sister is resting in the former first class smoking compartment with five seats. All seats became third class in 1941.

Plate 214: The BR Mark 1 coach designs were based upon Bulleid steam stock, but of all-steel construction. In appearance, the windows are squarer and there is no side-beading or roof stripping – see *plate 202* for a comparison. Set No. 535 looks immaculate, almost new, coupled incongruously behind SECR class H tank No. 31530 (some sixty years old). They are en route to Maidstone West on the dead-straight SER main line east of **Tonbridge**. SR lineside relics include the concrete ballast bin and fogman's hut, a 'distant' signal on a rail-built post and a platelayers' hut. The trunk telegraph is strung on two rows of poles to either side of the line.

Plate 217: All change at **Oxted**! Maunsell brake-composite No. 6681 (right) was built in 1935. A push-pull cab end was added in 1959 and set 602 was scrapped in 1963 (*Ref. 12*). Its front windows are much smaller than on pre-group conversions, having similar proportions to the new DMU No. 1311, seen here arriving from Victoria. The cab front of the latter incorporates fibreglass for the first time, eliminating sharp corners. There are also recesses for the connectors. This charming station has North Downs chalk quarries in the background and the platforms are adorned with SER arc canopies, SR 'barley sugar' lamp standards and Sugg Rochester gas lamps.

Plate 216: At **Hurst Green**, a Maunsell brake-third displays its small look-out ducket in the recessed end section. Note the side-bowing and those wonderful flat, flush windows. Developed from the LSWR's 'ironclad' stock (*plate 144*), coach No. 2837 dates from 1935. Always part of set 202, it was withdrawn in 1961 (*Ref. 12*).

Plate 215: The unprepossessing Hastings DMUs are instantly recognisable by their narrow front windows, '22' or '23' destination blinds, flat narrow sides, air louvres behind the cab and an ear-piercing roar from the engines. As an interim measure to replace pre-war 'Restriction 0' stock, they were originally intended to be steam-hauled. Instead, the end coaches were fitted with English Electric diesel-electric sets whose design had been proven in service in Egypt, but was new to BR. Built as 6-car units, they served East Sussex from 1957 until electrification in 1986. The open saloons were originally plushly upholstered in deep red with a gold 'chicken-wire' pattern. A young couple begin a 'day out on the Southern' as unit 1033 draws into the Down platform at **Sevenoaks**. This 12-car train would split at Tunbridge Wells, with a buffet car usually in the front fast half.

Plate 218: At **Dorking North**, the guard's ducket shows clearly on the side of 4-SUB unit No. 4510 of converted LBSCR steam stock (right). Alongside is unit 4102, the first type of Bulleid 4-SUB which was introduced in 1942 – identified by its domed roof end and round-cornered front windows. Both trains carry a headcode for the Waterloo to Horsham service, in letter and number form respectively. The Italianate LBSCR station building stands beyond, complemented by the large, flat platform canopies with heavy Gothic valancing.

Plate 219: EMU innovation was continuous under Richard Maunsell until his retirement in 1937. In that year, 4-car express units were introduced for the Portsmouth Direct services. They were the first with through-train corridors and gangways and were abbreviated to 4-COR and 4-RES (restaurant). Unit 3106 is seen at platform 12 at **Waterloo**, alongside Bulleid 0–6–0 class Q1 No. 33015 (on pilot duty). This wartime utility locomotive is some five years younger than the EMU. The end gangway is prominent, so too the headcode plate – Nelson's blind eye! Note the plain wooden island canopies, also the water crane and barrows on the right.

Plate 220: Photographed at **Herne Hill** on an Orpington to Victoria 4-SUB service, unit 4508 comprises coaches which were converted in the mid-1920s from old steam stock. The LBSCR low-arc roof profile, however, is disguised by the domed end. The cab end is standard SR, similar to the 2-BIL unit below, but narrower and lower. The BR colour-light signals have right-hand route indicators for the City line. A more recent addition is the single light seen on the left, which is presumably for entry into the Up Sorting Sidings next to the City line.

Plate 221: To complement the new electric express services to Brighton and the south coast, semi-fast EMUs were built in 2-car units with corridors but no inter-car gangway. Having two (bi-) lavatories, they were abbreviated to 2-BIL. Their external appearance is in many ways more attractive than the express units, having tall, flush corridor windows and traditional SR cab ends, bristling with cable connectors. There was one large window for the driver and a smaller opening window for changing the stencil-type headcode plate. Note also the guard's periscopes (instead of side-duckets), a development introduced by Maunsell and continued by Bulleid and BR. Unit 2092 is photographed at **Ore**, the EMU terminal. Note the SER arc roof canopy with ornate valancing.

Plate 222: The original EMUs of the LSWR and SR comprised 3-car driving units and 2-car trailing units. At peak times, they would operate in 3–2–3 formation, a practice phased out during the 1940s. One LSWR 3-SUB unit of 1915 vintage survived as Instruction Train S10, photographed in 1961 here at **Orpington**. It had a lecture room in one driving coach and a display of power control equipment in the trailer. The white roof end would once have extended along the whole train. The wooden panelling has all the elegance of the pre-group era. Indeed, this is LSWR steam stock, although it was extended from 1934 on new frames when SR steel ends were added

Plate 223: The earliest all-new EMUs of the SR appeared in 1925. They were steel-panelled throughout and featured LSWR-type bow ends. The motor coaches had seven passenger compartments compared with eight in plate 222 and five on the LSWR originals. From the early 1940s, 3-SUB units were progressively augmented with a trailer coach to become 4-SUB. Many such trailers were the wider Bulleid coaches, one of which is seen here at **Wimbledon** on unit 4312. The square panel behind the cab was formerly used for SR destination boards.

Plate 224: From 1960, a number of Bulleid trailers from 'augmented' 4-SUB units were converted into de-icing vans. DS 70050 is seen here at the **Peckham** depot in 1960. Both bogies have a boom for spray nozzles, with an inspection periscope above. Most of the doors have been removed and there is a 'ripple effect' of reflected rails where new panelling has been applied. Bulleid's rounded windows were a familiar suburban feature for several decades. See *plates 63* and *155* for Bulleid 4-SUB units, also *plate 40* for the later 4-EPB units of BR(S).

Plate 225: A Bulleid coach with a difference! In 1954, BR introduced a batch of cafeteria cars, a new concept incorporating a dining saloon at one end, a kitchen in the middle and a small cafeteria at the other. Most were allocated to LM Region, others were allocated to the Southern (used mainly on excursion and inter-Regional services). S9211E was photographed at **Portsmouth and Southsea** in 1959 and was scrapped in 1963. It was one of a batch of six converted at Eastleigh from ambulance cars which had seen service overseas during the Second World War (*Ref. 10*). They in turn had been converted from LNER third-class sleeping cars which had seven compartments of four berths, the top ones folding down for daytime use. Although the sides have new metal cladding and Southern accessories, the roof profile and bogie frames are distinctly LNER. It is a Gresley coach of 1928 vintage whose detail was the work of his personal assistant, none other than Oliver Bulleid.

Plate 226: The first Southern main line to be electrified was to Brighton in 1933, extended to Eastbourne and Hastings in 1936. Express EMUs of five Pullman, one Pullman or one pantry car were abbreviated to 5-BEL, 6-PUL and 6-PAN. The Pullman and motor coaches were of all-steel construction, but the ordinary trailers were wooden with steel panelling. Motor coach ends were flat-looking with domed roofs and almost square windows. Gangways were inter-car, but not inter-unit. Unlike other Maunsell stock, side windows were narrow and recessed. In a Victorian setting at **Hastings**, 6-PUL unit 3010 is seen departing beneath an ornate three-arch brick bridge. The balanced signal bracket is SR rail-built, carrying 'starting back' semaphores for platforms 3–4.

11 Locomotive Anthology

The Southern's electrification programme was put on hold for some two decades because of the Second World War. Pre-group and early SR steam locomotives were therefore granted an extended lease of life until the BR Modernisation Programme caught up. The final decade of Southern steam is therefore remarkable for its variety of steam locomotives, especially since they operated alongside the world's largest electrified suburban network.

This final chapter focuses upon steam locomotives in portrait, contrasting the old and the new, the large and the small, the sleek and the ungainly. The intention is to bring out the romance of engines in odd corners, rather than to describe their detail as a technical record (which plenty of authors have already done). After brief factual descriptions, the captions break into verse to portray the beauty of the beast and its setting and to emphasise certain mechanical detail. One of the secrets of digestible railway verse is to keep it short and to the point, so none herein exceeds six lines. So sit back and enjoy some 'poetry in motion' – although all but two of the pictures are of stationary locomotives! Take particular note of those designs which have been deliberately enhanced with fine lines or flares.

Finally, try to appreciate the technical and industrial genius of the individuals and teams responsible for engine concept, design and construction. Eight locomotive superintendents are represented here, all formidable characters who were masters of the latest technologies as well as brilliant administrators and man-managers. Remember too that they were responsible not only for new designs but for maintenance and modification of the old. Few classes escaped modification. Imagine the courage needed to rebuild the 'River' class 2–6–4 tanks as Mogul tender engines, or the postwar decision to rebuild the entire Pacific fleet. These portraits are a tribute to such giants of men and to all the ordinary people who supported them in drawing offices, locomotive works and running sheds.

Plate 227: At **Sydenham Hill**, Maunsell 4–4–0 'Schools' class V No. 30938, *St Olaves*, built in 1934:

St Olaves, the name of a church and a school
And an interwar loco – express engine pool;
Coasting through Sydenham Hill with a rake
Of crimson and cream BR coaches to take
To the havens of Margate and Ramsgate in Kent,
Of London and Chatham and Dover descent.

Modern and powerful, compact 4–4–0,
Three cylinders, one mighty chimney on show;
Footplate is stepped at the front and the rear,
Window and tender are angled but sheer.
Maunsell's small masterpiece, four-coupled charmer,
Protected by Saints – Olave, Saxby and Farmer.

Plate 228: At **Southampton Docks**, Bulleid 'West Country' class Pacific No. 34006, *Bude*, built in 1945:
A long way from Bude in a siding at rest, with water and ash but still looking its best;
Air-smoothed and shiny as was the intent, with nameplate and shield standing proud, redolent.
But what of the wingplates, exceedingly long? Alas, smoke deflection was what they got wrong!

Plate 229: At **Havant**, Stroudley 0–6–0 class A1X tank No. 32677, built in 1880 as LBSCR No. 77 *Wonersh* and reboilered by Marsh from 1911:

Neanderthal tank in the bay, from earlier railway epochs;
Bicycles, barrow and ash, a telephone call from the box;
Footbridge encased, office embraced,
Square Southern building, flat-roofed and brick-faced;
Watering time in the bay, our 'Terrier' held on the blocks.

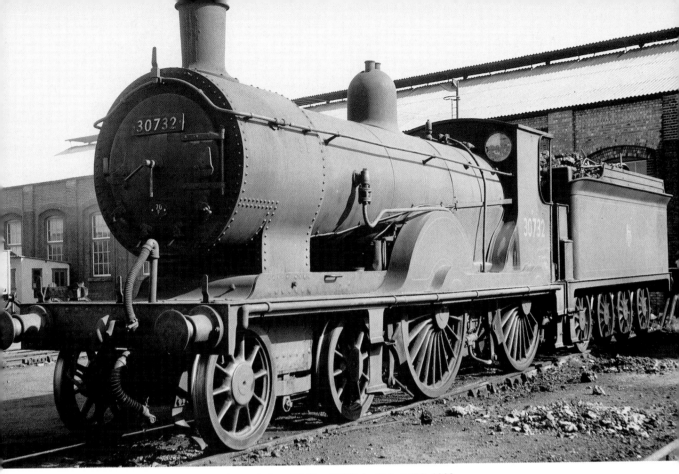

Plate 230: At **Fratton MPD**, Drummond 4–4–0 class T9 No. 30732, built in 1899–1900:
    Slender lines, continued through from buffer beam to tender;
    Thoroughbred, a Greyhound dame, what is your hidden splendour?
    Reciprocating parts inside, all wheels exposed – bespoken;
    Such grace – the man-size splasher box, its curvature unbroken.
    Clean-cut smokebox, stove-pipe hat, two 'safeties' on the steam dome;
    Square-cut cab, high tender rave – South-Western flair, Tee-ninedom!

Plate 231: At **Sandown**, Adams 0–4–4 class O2 tanks Nos. 22, 20, 30 and 29, built during 1889–95:
 O, to be in Sandown in nineteen fifty-nine; 0–4–4s a-plenty, stored on the Newport line;
 O, for all the little trains puffing down from Ryde; William Adams' O2 tanks with nameplates on the side;
 O, before the Underground, humming on the track; *Brading*, number twenty-two, so clean and shining black;
 Old South-Western engines, standing in a row; proud Southern island enclave – to thee so much we owe.

Plate 232: At **Ryde Works**, Adams 0–4–4 class O2 tank, unidentified, built during 1889–95:
Island workshop, light and airy, does your workload ever vary?
Tyre repairs and smoke-tubes too, seen here in this general view.
Wheel the barrow, swing the crane, stoke the forge and fire again!
Clear the anvil, close the vice, drop the hammer once or twice!
Busy workshop, hot and cold, belonging to the days of old.

Plate 233: At **Exeter Central**, Maunsell 0–8–0 class Z tank No. 30952, built in 1929:
Parties of eight save five bob in the pound, so travel by train to be sure!
The Exeter banker, ungainly but clean, displayed for our eyes to explore:
Tri-level footplate, eight-coupled wheels, a bunker in Queen Mary class;
High cab-roof, low window, a sloping tank-top, bent bars for the spectacle glass.
Stand by your standpipe and top up your tanks, open the cylinder drain!
Rest on your laurels and fill up with tea, ready for banking again!

Plate 234: At **Exmouth Junction MPD**, Bulleid 'Merchant Navy' class Pacific No. 35001, *Channel Packet*, built in 1941 and rebuilt in 1959:

> Southern swan-song, masterpiece of steam re-engineering;
> Fresh from Eastleigh's loco shops, dark green and most endearing;
> Nameplate roundel, boxpok wheels, added weights for balance,
> Walschaerts valve gear, one of three, with access for maintenance;
> Smoke deflectors, large and proud, handrails down the casing;
> Low-cut tender, once so tall; great firebox, all embracing.

Plate 235: At **Three Bridges**, Wainwright 0–4–4 class H tank No. 31161, built in 1909:

> Wainwright and wheelwright, carpenters few; blacksmith and foundryman, riveters too;
> To fine railway company workshops they came, 'South Eastern and Chatham' and 'Brighton', by name.
> Fifty years on in a Three Bridges bay, their products are worked by the crew of the day,
> Filling the water-tanks, damping the coal – shadows at eventide, no other soul;
> But the ghosts of the craftsmen who moulded this train give joy to the traveller, time and again.

Plate 236 (*opposite*): At **Hayling Island**, Stroudley 0–6–0 'Terrier' class A1X tank No. 32677, built in 1880:

Stroudley cab-side, aperture square,
Rounded corners – debonaire!
Tapered handrails, shiny bright knobs;
Splasher worn by crewmen's hobs;
Hanging steam-pump, thick with black paint,
Rise and fall for brake restraint.

Round-topped side-tank, yellow-red lines;
Regulator handle shines;
Open fire-hole, smooth timber floor;
Reversing lever, gauges four;
Salter 'safeties' linked to the dome;
Brighton 'Terrier' – South Coast home.

Plate 237: At **Fratton MPD**, Maunsell class U Mogul No. 31808, built in 1925 as 2–6–4 class K tank No. 808 *River Char* and rebuilt in 1928:

Simple Southern workhorse with a Belpaire firebox, modestly attired but elegantly bred;
Daughter of a river, a Dorset Charmer, awaits a turn of duty at a south coast shed.

Plate 238: At **Marland Moor** (south of Torrington) Ivatt 2–6–2 class 2MT tank No. 41295, built in 1951:
Wandering minstrel of LMS build, bringing the empties from far afield;
Tapering bunker and spectacle plate, china-clay siding with multi-bar gate;
Ivatt the engineman – Stevenson's heir; Stephens the line-builder – railway corsair;
Wandering branch that the Southern restored; glorious Devon and Cornwall's lost cord.

Plate 239: At **Gravesend**, Wainwright 0–4–4 class H tank No. 31263, built in 1905:
Sixteen tons of best Welsh coal, a wagon-load of fuel;
Manual coaling (pile it high!), beside the local school;
Pagoda roof, a bunker flare – Edwardian finesse;
But three more tons of clinkered ash can make an awful mess!

Index of Photographic Locations